Accession no
3
D1392107

Talent Management in Education

Education at SAGE

SAGE is a leading international publisher of journals, books, and electronic media for academic, educational, and professional markets.

Our education publishing includes:

- accessible and comprehensive texts for aspiring education professionals and practitioners looking to further their careers through continuing professional development
- inspirational advice and guidance for the classroom
- authoritative state of the art reference from the leading authors in the field

Find out more at: **www.sagepub.co.uk/education**

Talent Management in Education

Brent Davies and

Barbara J. Davies

LIS LIBRARY

Date 13/4/11. | Fund e.

Order No WITHDRAWN 2189835

University of Chester

SAGE

Los Angeles | London | New Delhi
Singapore | Washington DC

© Brent Davies and Barbara J. Davies 2011
First published 2011

Apart from any fair dealing for the purposes of research or
private study, or criticism or review, as permitted under the
Copyright, Designs and Patents Act 1988, this publication may
be reproduced, stored or transmitted in any form, or by any
means, only with the prior permission in writing of the
publishers, or in the case of reprographic reproduction, in
accordance with the terms of licences issued by the Copyright
Licensing Agency. Enquiries concerning reproduction outside
those terms should be sent to the publishers.

SAGE Publications Ltd
1 Oliver's Yard
55 City Road
London EC1Y 1SP

SAGE Publications Inc.
2455 Teller Road
Thousand Oaks, California 91320

SAGE Publications India Pvt Ltd
B 1/I 1 Mohan Cooperative Industrial Area
Mathura Road
New Delhi 110 044

SAGE Publications Asia-Pacific Pte Ltd
33 Pekin Street #02–01
Far East Square
Singapore 048763

Library of Congress Control Number: 2010929993

British Library Cataloguing in Publication data
A catalogue record for this book is available from the British
Library

ISBN 978-0-85702-734-4
ISBN 978-0-85702-737-5 (pbk)

Typeset by Dorwyn, Wells, Somerset
Printed in Great Britain by CPI Antony Rowe, Chippenham, Wiltshire
Printed on paper from sustainable resources

This book is dedicated to the memory of our talented fathers:

Ken Davies and John Gray

Contents

List of figures

Acknowledgements

The authors and the publisher would like to thank the following for permission to use material in the book:

Robertson, A. and Abbey, G. *Clued Up: Working Through Politics and Complexity*, 2001, Pearson Education Limited, for the use of Figure 8.1.

Peters, T. *Talent*, 2005, reproduced by permission of Penguin Books Ltd.

The authors also wish to acknowledge the following educators who have contributed to our thinking and helped us to translate theory into practice:

Wendy Allen
Mark Bennison
Jane Bowman
Mary Bolton
David Carter
Martin Coles
Trevor Clarke
Barry Day
Jeff Dawkins
Cathy Deegan
Paula Elston
Lynn Gladd
Jody Goldsworthy
Zoe Goodwin
Howard Green
David Hopkins
Karen Igoea
Esther Kendell
Lesley King
John King

David Lamper
Mark Lofthouse
Julia Newton
Hilary Macaulay
Linda Marshall
Tony Mackay
Dan Moynihan
Lynn O'Neill
Kevin Orr
David Porrit
Stephen Swailes
Alan Thomas
Ken Thompson
Gayle Thorpe
David Triggs
Julie Wallis
Jonathan Wainwright
Bill Watkin
Graham Wright

About the authors

Dr Brent Davies, Cert Ed, BA, MSc, MPhil, PhD. Dr Brent Davies is Professor of Leadership Development at the University of Hull. He is also a Professorial Fellow at the University of Melbourne, a Special Professor at the University of Nottingham and a Faculty Member of the Centre on Educational Governance at the University of Southern California. Brent spent the first ten years of his career working as a teacher in South London. He then moved into higher education and now works exclusively on leadership and management development programmes for senior and middle managers in schools. Brent was Head of Education Leadership at Crewe and Alsager College of Higher Education and then moved to be the Director of the International MBA in School Leadership at Leeds Metropolitan University. He was appointed to the University of Lincolnshire and Humberside to establish the first Chair in Educational Leadership and create the International Educational Leadership Centre in Lincoln. In 2000, at the University of Hull he established the International Leadership Centre. In 2004, he moved within the University to become a research professor in leadership development at the Hull University Business School.

He has published extensively, including 30 books and 80 articles on leadership and management. His recent books include: *Leading the Strategically Focused Schoool* (2nd edition, 2011, Sage), *Developing Successful Leadership* (2010, Springer), *Essentials of School Leadership*, 2nd edition (2009, Sage), *Passionate Leadership* (with Tim Brighouse, 2008, Sage), *Developing Sustainable Leadership* (2007, Sage), *Strategic Marketing for Schools* (2007, Beijing Normal University Press), *Leading the Strategically Focused School* (2006, Sage), *Naujoji Strategine Kryptis Ir Mokyklos Pletre* (2006, Vilnus: Homo libre), *The Essentials of School Leadership* (2005, Sage), *School Leadership in the 21st Century* (2005, Routledge), *The New Strategic Direction and Development of the School* (2003, Routledge-Falmer) and *The Handbook of Educational Leadership and Management*

(2003, Pearson). Brent was also co-director and author of the NCSL research project and report 'Success and Sustainability: Developing the Strategically Focused School' (2005, NCSL). www.brentdavies.co.uk

Dr Barbara J. Davies, Cert Ed, BEd, MA, EdD. Dr Barbara Davies has extensive experience in primary school leadership and management. After graduating from Oxford University, Barbara taught in primary schools in Oxfordshire, Germany and West Sussex. She took up her first headship in West Sussex followed by her second in North Yorkshire. She was a senior lecturer at Bishop Grosseteste College in Lincoln, working in initial teacher education, before specialising in leadership and management in the primary sector at the University of Lincolnshire and Humberside, where she was a course leader for a masters degree in leadership and learning. Subsequently, she returned to primary headship in Nottinghamshire before taking up her fourth headship in Lincolnshire from 2001 until 2008. Barbara gained a masters degree in Educational Management in 1994 with the Open University and a Doctorate in Educational Leadership at the University of Hull in 2004. Her thesis focused on strategic leadership and planning in primary schools. She has published a number of books and articles in the field of educational leadership. Barbara is currently a researcher in the business school of the University of Hull working on a number of educational leadership projects.

The Context

Chapter 1

Introduction

This chapter considers:

> the definition of talent
> talent for future schools
> the nature of leadership
> a model for leadership
> the major themes and structure of the book.

Background

Talent management is increasingly seen as a critical factor in developing successful organisations and is a strategic priority for businesses. It is just as critical a factor for schools. Indeed, in a people-focused organisation such as a school, the key resource is the talent of the individuals who work there. In education, the 'talent' could be considered as the critical factor in school success. We would prefer to use the term talent leadership as it expresses what the whole process is about. However, common practice uses the phrase talent management and for ease of use we have followed this convention in the book. The growing leadership skill shortage, difficulty in appointing head teachers (and other senior/middle leaders) and the work–life-balance agenda is leading to a shortage of people who are capable of making a difference to organisational performance. A focus on talent management will contribute to other strategic objectives, such as building a high-performance learning environment and building leadership in depth in the school. This is different from simple succession planning and filling typical hierarchical leadership roles that exist today, as it is a process of providing able and talented people who will create new and different leadership roles in the future.

This is particularly important for schools which are facing the challenge of developing innovative and imaginative leaders to meet the needs of school transformation. Individual schools need to develop a talent pool and to co-operate with other schools for cross-institutional development of leadership and curriculum talent. This is of significant interest to trusts, all-through schools, academy groups, federated schools and school network groups and school 'brands' where staff can be presented with a coherent developmental strategy, which may include planned work opportunities with different schools in the network. New staff or middle leaders could be provided with leadership opportunities across the institutions, such as award-bearing qualifications and in-house learning to systematically enhance the talent pool within the group.

It is not enough to attract people with high potential, there must be a planned strategy for managing their talents which is supported by processes to retain the commitment of talented people and properly use their abilities. The ability to attract and retain high-quality individuals is a key leadership challenge as the school community moves forward.

Definition

There are many views on the nature of talent. The Chartered Institute of Personnel and Development state:

> *Talent consists of those individuals who can make a difference to organisational performance, either through their immediate contribution or in the longer term by demonstrating the highest levels of potential.* (CIPD, 2007)

Talent management is defined as a systematic and dynamic process of discovering, developing and sustaining talented individuals. What works in the talent management process depends on the context and the way the organisation implements practices. So talent management may be organisational specific and dependent on the context but could be defined as:

> *Talent management is the systematic attraction, identification, development, engagement/retention and deployment of those individuals with high potential who are of particular value to an organisation.* (CIPD, 2006)

Talent for future schools

One of the key reasons for taking a talent management perspective is that leaders need to focus on the staffing needs of their schools as they move forward into the future and not simply to concern themselves with simple succession planning of existing roles. In doing so, leaders need to address the following questions:

1. What will schools of the future look like?
2. How do we view leadership for these future schools?
3. What are the characteristics of future leaders?

1. What will schools of the future look like?

This involves several ideas all starting from a consideration of the nature and dimensions of learning and how we need to construct human, organisational and structural arrangements to maximise the learning potential of each child. Initiatives such as Building Schools of the Future (BSF) and the new Academy Buildings have to not just represent 'best practice' but 'new practice' if a 'once in a generation' opportunity to refurbish and rebuild learning centres for our children is to be fully exploited. Most importantly, we should question how we lead and manage within those new building structures to create a successful framework for learning. Linking physical, structural, learning and leadership design needs talented individuals who can think 'outside the box'.

The establishment of the Every Child Matters (ECM) agenda in England and the consequent establishment of Children's Services, which draws together a number of departments of education and social provision for children, has radically altered how we view schools. Instead of isolated units just looking after the education of a group of children in catchment areas, schools are now at the centre of a network of services which attempt to coordinate provision for children and young people.

The provision of education has traditionally been a public sector responsibility with the small additional provision by independent schools. Within the public sector, state education has been just that, state education. Although the private sector would be commissioned to build schools or provide materials such as textbooks, their role was limited. Increasingly during the 1990s and with greater pace during the first decade of the 21st century, the role of the private sector as a provider and deliverer of public sector education has grown exponentially. Private sector organisations run schools on behalf of the state and local authority services are contracted out to private sector companies. Organisations are encouraged to establish groups of secondary schools or secondary school brands under the expansion of the Academy programme and the 'free schools' initiative with direct funding from central government thus by-passing local authority funding and local authority control.

The impact of technology has allowed students to be off-site or have multiple-site delivery of education which changes the way we conceptualise 'school' from a building to a process in a number of venues and locations with a number of delivery mechanisms. In considering talent development for future schools, we need to encompass a debate along these lines.

2. How do we view leadership for these future schools?

Consideration of this question clearly needs an understanding of the key elements of leadership but this needs to be understood in the context of new patterns of leadership. These patterns include executive leadership, hard and soft federations, school groups and providers, co-leadership and shared leadership patterns. This new re-conceptualisation of leadership and school configurations under the broad title of system leadership is re-writing the traditional picture of school leadership. If these ideas are built onto our existing knowledge of distributed leadership, this does indeed force a radical rethink of leadership for schools in the future. Certainly, a leader in the future will need to be both innovative and entrepreneurial. This encompasses the need to transform the learning and teaching process by looking at innovative practice but also the means of acquiring and utilising resources needs a different mindset from that of the traditional educational leader. It is important, as we have discussed above, to encompass systems leadership within a networked relationship with other providers. We will develop this idea next.

3. What are the characteristics of future leaders?

Talent management is the process of looking for individuals with the potential to lead, which is the focus for succeeding chapters, but it is worth emphasising that current performance is not the same as potential for future leadership, which may be a substantially different role. We suggest that these roles are likely to involve the ability to:

➣ be change champions
➣ be leaders of innovation

➤ be flexible and able to live with ambiguity
➤ grasp opportunities and be entrepreneurial.

The Hay Group (2008) see the change in leadership from formal management approaches to connected leadership approaches in the 21st century as follows:

Formal management	**Connected leadership**
Vertical	Horizontal
Hierarchical	Collegiate
Instruction	Dialogue
Constrained	Flexible
One-way	Two-way
Accountability	Reciprocity
Robust	Fragile
History irrelevant	History matters
Control of resource	Creation of trust

Figure 1.1   *The difference between connected leadership roles and traditional management posts (Hay Group, 2008: 9)*

This figure shows how we can reconceptualise leadership for future schools from the more traditional approach to connected leadership.

Changing organisational culture

Current development culture ⟷	**Talent management culture**
Benchmark current practice	Be ahead of the curve
Reliable employees	Creative, challenging employees
Predictable promotion structures	New and different school structures
A job	A high performance role
Risk adverse	Adventuresome

Figure 1.2   *Current and future leaders (adapted from Peters, 2005: 131)*

Writers in the leadership literature tend to use ideas like those in Figure 1.2 to articulate the shift in organisational culture from a succession approach to a talent management approach.

So what does a potential leader look like?

Much has been written about leadership through the lenses of frameworks, tools and processes. We want to identify the essential aspects that dominate the debate about what effective leaders do in order to create a model which will give structure and guidance to our book. This model is necessary in order to help people conceptualise how to be better leaders and help those responsible for building better leadership. We offer a way of *thinking about* being a better leader and *being* a better leader. Both are necessary for the identification and development of potential leaders.

We believe that in being an effective leader you must start with yourself. Leaders need to model the behaviour they require from others and model what they want others to know. Effective leaders have a responsibility to help others to lead. If you lead well, success can be ensured for the present, and future success is secured if you enable others to learn the principles to lead well. We need some sort of structure and guidance and our model, in Figure 1.3, is a way of thinking about being a better leader and how to build better leadership aptitude.

The debate as to whether leaders are born or made is interesting and pertinent to the focus of this book. Adair (2006: 41) believes that 'the idea that leaders are born and not made is only half the truth'. We agree and believe that leaders may be 'half born' and have personal qualities, thoughts and natural abilities but experience, learning and practice provide the 'made' half. 'It takes a long time to become a natural leader' (Adair, 2006: 41). All leaders can become better, whatever their natural ability. If leadership drives action, then it is important to establish what we need people to get better at and use those elements to evaluate potential and how that potential will be developed. A potential leader could be a natural leader in one aspect of our model, for example their personal qualities. It would be unusual for this expertise to extend automatically to the other elements of the model. The potential leader may have mastery in these areas but could develop expertise if they are given the appropriate opportunities and experiences to learn.

It is easy to generate long lists of excellent ideas in order to answer 'What makes an effective leader?' Just ask your colleagues! We agree with the ideas listed in Figures 1.1 and 1.2 and would add that leaders need to build high-performing teams, need to ensure accountability, need to be emotionally intelligent, need to be able to communicate effectively and actively live the core values such as honesty and trust. We want to build an holistic framework to cover the landscape of leadership, to identify the key elements of what makes an effective leader. This will help us to identify potential leaders and enable leaders to get better. This we do next in our leadership model (Figure 1.3).

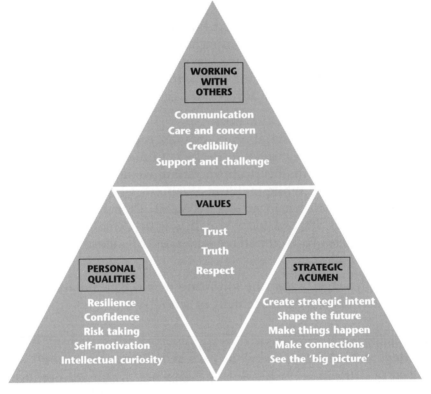

Figure 1.3 *Key dimensions of leadership*

First, it is important to establish the need to be a *strategist*, and this forms the *first element* in our model. It is important for a leader to set the future direction for the school – being strategic is a way of managing the impact of future trends and influences on the school and being able to make conscious decisions about those influences. It is about setting priorities and using resources to achieve those priorities.

Strategic leaders need to care about others in order to want to involve them. Individual leaders can make a difference but for sustainable organisations strength comes from staff working together to achieve the same goals (Barth, 1990). Leaders need to understand their school, those in the school community and those in the wider community (Davies, 2004). Understanding the school context and having *people skills* forms the *second element* of our model. Talent managers nurture and develop others, and get the best out of their colleagues. They find ways to engage others and feel a sense of personal contribution to a school's development.

The *third key element* of our model is the leader's *personal qualities*. What leaders know and do is important but who they are also determines what they can achieve. Most importantly, effective leaders motivate loyalty and support because of the way they behave, conducting themselves with integrity and trust. Effective leaders have the confidence to work with people who are, or have the ability to become, better than themselves.

We have mentioned moral standards as central to each of these elements, which is why *values* form the central element of our model. Values should be at the heart of everything we do, both organisationally and personally. While building a values framework is important, that they must be seen in action is critical. Each key element has a number of processes and ideas which will be explored in the forthcoming chapters. Each chapter enables us to identify a leadership challenge.

Our research suggests that the following would be a suitable template for considering talent management in schools:

Defining organisational strategy and values	Where are you going and what type of people do you want to help you to get there?
Talent identification	Evaluate your people: performance evaluation and performance challenge as a core activity.
Talent development	Establish powerful professional learning; develop structures to facilitate the process.
Talent culture	Become an employer of choice and create a success culture.
The way forward	Create a way forward through an integrated talent management model for the school.

Figure 1.4   *The major themes of the book*

How these themes are developed through the individual chapters can be seen as follows:

The structure of the book

The Context
1 Introduction
2 Defining organisational strategy and values

Section 1 – Talent Identification
3 Performance evaluation
4 Performance or potential?

Section 2 – Talent Development
5 Talent development
6 Professional learning
7 The architecture to support talent development

Section 3 – Talent Culture
8 Building a talent-management culture
9 School or system talent?

The Way Forward
10 An integrated talent-management model for schools

Chapter outlines

All the chapters will explain the key concepts and provide frameworks for leaders to apply the ideas in their organisation. This practical application of the theory will be enhanced through insights from practice and vignettes of exemplary shareable practice.

The context

1. Introduction

This chapter will explore the nature and dimensions of talent management and explains the difference between succession planning, defined as 'preparing people for current jobs', and talent management seen as 'developing talented individuals for the changing nature of schools in the future'. The chapter establishes a leadership model for talent management.

2. Defining organisational strategy and values

If you cannot define the values on which your organisation is based and where your organisation wants to go, then recruiting individuals who will fit your value set and culture and who will want to join you in your leadership journey is very difficult! This chapter looks at defining strategy and values as the bedrock of all leadership and management processes including talent management.

Section 1 Talent identification

3. Performance evaluation

The first stage in talent management is evaluating the talent already evident in the school, developing a staffing map and defining staffing needs for the present and the future. This involves critical and honest judgements and conversations with all members of staff. It is too easy to see this as only necessary to address the problem of underperformance, and while this is vital so is challenging all levels of performance and providing a framework for all to improve. It is critically important to identify the small group of highly talented individuals who will contribute to a high-performing and sustainable school of the future.

4. Performance or potential?

One of the most critical dimensions of talent management is to be able to distinguish between the current performance of the individual and the future potential to undertake a leadership role. Current performance is not necessarily a good measure of future potential. This chapter will examine this dilemma leading into factors to support identification, which will be discussed in the next chapter.

Section 2 Talent development

5. Talent development

This chapter looks at how effective schools develop leadership by initially providing frameworks for the individual and the school to evaluate leadership skills. It then looks at a variety of learning activities which can develop leadership talent. It proposes a five-stage process to deepen the understanding of leadership development and how these might be configured as stages in leadership enhancement.

6. Professional learning

In this chapter, we consider the establishment of a framework for learning skills, behaviours and opportunities that promote leadership development. Critical to this process is the concept of leaders as lead learners. The chapter goes on to consider the sort of learning opportunities that develop leadership potential and how schools can develop a culture of leadership learning.

7. The architecture to support talent development

This chapter will consider how schools could set up the architecture for identifying talent, recording talent development and outlining future needs from an organisational and an individual perspective. It will present major case studies of the approaches of a primary school and a secondary school.

Section 3 Talent culture

8. Building a talent-management culture

If sustainable development is to be achieved for each individual member of staff and the school as an organisation, then a talent management culture needs to exist across the organisation. This chapter will highlight what successful practice looks like, with case examples from several schools which exemplify what a talent culture 'feels' and 'looks' like. This involves becoming a talent developer and engager. This chapter will also be concerned with the central question of how an individual school can become an 'employer of choice', where there will be a pool of individuals wanting to work for the school and where the school is able to retain and sustain talent.

9. School or system talent?

This chapter will address whether individual schools can develop their own talent systems or whether partnerships or federations are needed to maximise opportunities such as 'managed moves' and school-based award-bearing activities.

The way forward

10. An integrated talent-management model for schools

The threads of the book will be drawn together in this final chapter and present an action plan for schools to move forward in this exciting and innovative area.

Suggested further reading

CIPD (2006) *Talent Management: Understanding the Dimensions.* London: CIPD.

CIPD (2007) *Talent: Strategy, Management, Measurement.* London: CIPD.

Cross, A. (2007) *Talent Management Pocketbook.* Alresford, Hants: Management Pocketbooks Ltd.

Peters, T. (2005) *Talent: Develop it, Sell it, Be it.* London: Dorling Kindersley.

An initial reflection

Throughout the book, we have used a number of reflection points, evaluations, questions and inventories. As a starting point, readers may wish to discuss the following inventory with a colleague to evaluate their current talent development practice. If you score five for each question, you may think that you do not need to read the book!

Where are you now with talent management?

For each statement below, indicate how accurately the statement describes your school.

'1' indicates 'rarely', on a graded scale to '5' which indicates 'always'.

1. We have a clearly articulated set of core values.	1 2 3 4 5
2. The values are demonstrated in daily behaviours.	1 2 3 4 5
3. We have a strategic plan which includes talent development.	1 2 3 4 5
4. We have an effective performance management process which supports the identification of talent.	1 2 3 4 5
5. We are able to discriminate between current performance and future potential of staff.	1 2 3 4 5
6. We can map the behaviours, skills and attitudes which need to be developed in potential leaders.	1 2 3 4 5
7. Our professional learning includes specific opportunities to develop leadership potential.	1 2 3 4 5
8. We have pathways, programmes and processes to facilitate the development of talent.	1 2 3 4 5
9. Our culture enables the celebration of everyone's contribution	1 2 3 4 5
10. We work in partnership with others to develop talent in a more effective way.	1 2 3 4 5

Chapter 2

Defining organisational strategy and values

This chapter considers:

➤ developing a strategic approach
➤ the characteristics of strategic talent development
➤ defining and developing values in a school
➤ values and the leader.

It is important to define the values on which your organisation is based and define where your organisation wants to go, then recruiting individuals who will fit into your value set and culture and who will want to join you in your leadership journey is very difficult!

Why a strategic approach?

A major challenge for leaders in schools is to both address the short-term organisational imperatives and to build a longer-term strategic framework through which to develop the school into new and exciting areas. Clearly, you cannot develop future leadership talent if you do not have a view of where the school is going and have a framework that allows the school to plan and enact that journey. So initially basic questions such as, 'Where are we going?', 'What sort of organisation do we want to be?' and 'What will be the key factors in our successful development?' need to be answered and need to be part of the strategy-building process. It is only when this strategic vision and framework exists that matching talent to the needs of the school can begin.

In defining a strategic approach, a useful way of thinking about strategy can be encapsulated in five concepts. The first concerns the desired nature of the school in the future. This is trying to answer

'Where are we going and what sort of school do we want to be?' In attempting to confront these issues, it is essential to consider what sort of individuals and teams we need to enable us to move forward and develop into that sort of organisation.

The second concept relates to a time frame. Here, it is useful to consider that operational decisions take a one- to two-year time frame whereas strategy involves a three- to five-year time frame. This is important if we are trying to develop strategic talent. It requires a focus on developing individuals for the organisation of the future and gives the school time to build that capacity. There is always the danger of 'solutionalism', for example considering what the problem is and what the solution would be in terms of finding instant answers. It is more important to think in terms of what the challenges are and how we build capacity to fully understand the nature and dimensions of those challenges. Then we should move on to consider what we need to do to address that challenge and how we need to change in order to be able to do so.

The third concept concerns the ability to keep a broad perspective of the nature of future developments. We have said earlier that what organisations need to do is to recruit and develop talented individuals and mould and adapt their organisational roles to fully utilise their talents. This is different from saying in five years' time we need someone with a specific skill set to replace an existing defined role after someone retires. The nature and shape of the organisation are evolving and changing and we need to incorporate broad themes of these changes and not get over-concerned with the minutiae of incremental planning.

Fourth, strategy should provide a link between short-term and medium-term planning in that a strategic framework or approach should provide a template against which to judge short-term actions. If there is not a sense of strategic direction, then it is impossible to assess whether short-term actions are contributing to longer-term goals.

Fifth, strategy should be a means of marshalling and directing resources to the achievement of organisational goals. It should enable an organisation to focus on its key activities and determine how to prioritise resources to achieve them. Central to this strategic focus is the development of the talented individuals in order to contribute to the achievement of those strategic goals. Clearly, you need to know where you are going in order to know which people you need to get you there. If you do know where you want to get to, there is a better chance of enabling the right set of people to work towards that goal.

In determining a strategy, it is possible to use a number of approaches. One is strategic planning. Strategic planning is a rational, linear and predictable approach to setting the direction of the school. It assumes you know what you want to achieve, what stages you need to go through and what the outcome will be. This can be summarised as 'who does what?', 'when?' and 'how?' and 'how do we know when it has been done?' The key to successful strategic planning is a focused approach so that a school concentrates on four or five major themes (Davies, 2011). While this is a valuable approach, it has its limitations. One of the ways of coping with the limitations is to build an emergent strategy process into the more linear approach of strategic planning. Emergent strategy is a reactive and reflective approach to changes within the environment. As events and requirements change, so leadership teams need to make sense of those changes and new strategies and approaches emerge. Thus, the original strategic plan is amended and changed as the organisation moves forward in a changing environment.

Schools deal with some challenges that are multi-dimensional and complex. While they may know the desired outcome they want to achieve, they may not fully understand the nature and dimensions of the strategic challenge and may need to build a fuller understanding before they can move forward. This is where strategic leaders demonstrate their creativity by setting strategic intents and building capacity to first fully understand the nature and dimensions of the challenge and then seeking information and examples of excellent practice elsewhere to build and create a new way of tackling the challenge before moving on to a more formal planning state. Strategic intents are often concerned with raising the achievement of the school in difficult areas which often involves deep-seated cultural attitudes in the school. Examples would be moving from a simple incremental school improvement approach to one which creates a high achievement and success culture where students believe they can achieve, where staff expect more of the children and the community and parents are re-engaged as active supporters of their children's education. This involves complex levels of understanding and building a way of moving forward. Effective strategic leaders operate on the rational side by creating strategic plans although adjusting them with emergent strategy insights, while at the same time creating strategic intents which will enable the school to make strategic leaps in performance in areas which need radical reform and change. This can be summarised by the ABCD model in Figure 2.1:

Articulate	1	Current understanding and desired new strategy
Build	2	Images Metaphors Experiences of desired new understanding
Create	3	Dialogue and conversations Shared understanding to frame new understandings
Define	4	Establish formal plans and frame of reference for the school

Figure 2.1 *The ABCD model (Davies, 2011)*

The key strategic leadership attribute is to be able to move though the first three stages, in Figure 2.1, of building strategic intents before defining the final plan. With strategic planning, it is possible to move straight to level 4, however sustainable strategic change which encompasses complex problems, necessitates building a culture of understanding and involvement before that level 4 planning and implementation can begin. This capacity change is one of the significant differences between a strategic and an operational leader.

In building a strategic direction for the school, it is important that a strategic framework exists so that a talent map can be established. This means that the appropriate individuals can be recruited and/or developed to meet those longer-term organisational needs. While in many cases this can be seen as a rational and even linear process so that key staff attributes and abilities can be defined and developed, it is not always the case. The creativity that organisations need to define and meet the challenge of strategic intents often needs divergent thinkers who can cope with complexity and cultural change. In this case, having the creative leadership talent may be more important than having individuals who can fulfil specific positions within the organisation. The following diagnostic inventory is worth considering to support your review of your strategic leadership skills.

How strategic is your leadership?

For each statement below, indicate how accurately the statement describes you. '1' indicates 'rarely,' on a graded scale to '5' which indicates 'always'.

1. I balance the longer-term view with shorter-term operational pressures. 1 2 3 4 5

2. I take a 'helicopter view' and rise above everyday operational detail. 1 2 3 4 5

3. I compare the potential short- and long-term consequences of actions I'm considering. 1 2 3 4 5

4. I understand the difference between strategic planning and strategic intent. 1 2 3 4 5

5. I look for opportunities today that might generate valuable results tomorrow. 1 2 3 4 5

6. I question my own long-standing assumptions and encourage others to question theirs. 1 2 3 4 5

7. I can turn strategy into action. 1 2 3 4 5

8. I can involve staff groups in strategic conversations. 1 2 3 4 5

9. I understand how the wider political and cultural environment affects my organisation. 1 2 3 4 5

10. I can mobilise others to achieve strategic objectives. 1 2 3 4 5

Characteristics of strategic talent developers

The ability to build strategic plans and create strategic intents is necessary if a strategic framework is to be established upon which a talent development framework can be built. The leaders of a school also need to display and enact other strategic leadership skills and attributes. We would highlight three: (i) strategic talent developers are strategic thinkers; (ii) strategic talent developers are strategic learners; and (iii) strategic talent developers exert strategic influence. We will look at each of these qualities in turn.

(i) Strategic talent developers are strategic thinkers. It is vital to think of strategy as aligned to strategic thinking as a means of developing a strategic perspective rather than just the traditional view of strategy being linked to mechanistic strategic plans. What are the activities that a strategic leader has to engage in to develop this strategic perspective? The first is scanning. This involves scanning the environment in its political, economic and educational dimensions to identify ideas and trends that will impact on the school in the succeeding years so that strategic leaders can identify them and devise approaches to utilise them and position the school to maximise its future opportunities. The second is envisioning a new and desirable future for the school based on the information gained from the scanning process and relating that to the school's capacity to change and develop. The third is reframing the process, of setting the new future in context and finally making sense of that for the staff and students of the school. This often involves engaging in a strategic process and building new mental models.

During this process of strategic thinking, strategic leaders engage in synthesis as well as analysis. The importance of this is not to break everything down into its component parts and risk 'paralysis by analysis' but to see how the components can fit together and build an integrated successful whole. Effective schools have a success culture which is an integration of a number of elements built up over a period of time. It is this synthesis of good ideas and outstanding practice that creates a success culture. What is needed, very often, is nonlinear as well as linear thinking. Strategic leaders are able to think 'outside the box' and engage in tangential thinking that can incorporate new and innovative ways of doing things. It moves away from the step-by-step incremental approach and breaks new ground by considering alternative possibilities. Strategic thinking engages the heart as well as the head. It involves the values and beliefs of the strategic leader, which are implicit in the way they think, as much as the more public explanations of policy. Finally, strategic thinking can be visual as well as verbal. The systems thinking concept of rich pictures (Jackson, 2003) is useful here. Consider what a great school would look like – how could you see it in terms of its buildings and the interactions of its people? One of the key talents of strategic leaders is that they are able to create rich pictures of the future which individuals can see and understand and so they become part of the collective imagination of what is possible in the future.

(ii) Strategic talent developers are strategic learners. If the leader is not constantly seeking new knowledge and insights, they fail to move the organisation on and importantly fail to provide a model for staff and students. If the leader cannot be a strategic learner, there is little chance that defining the talent needed for the future can be defined and developed. Hughes and Beatty (2005: 74) adapt work from systems theory and apply it to how strategic leaders can learn. Learning for strategic leaders may involve:

➤ Looking at the big picture – what can I learn from the broader environment?

➤ Looking for patterns over time – how can I learn from data and seek patterns in the data so as to extract useful information?

➤ Looking for complex interactions – how can I synergise and learn from interrelationships?

➤ Understanding what causes what – learning that it may be more complex than it seems.

➤ Making time for reflection on models, theories and experiences.

Strategic leaders do not leave learning to chance; they set up the organisational framework to ensure it happens for themselves and others. A good way to look at this is to consider organisational culture, structure and systems which support strategic learning.

Organisational culture sets the tone for how learning is thought of in the school. The culture should be one where learning is seen as integral to the leadership role in order to develop and improve, not something that is a one-off and where once it has been achieved there is nothing more to learn. Is the learning culture that of knowledge transfer, something that you learn and pass on or something that you enquire about and develop and share? These cultural frameworks often reflect the difference between shallow knowledge and deep learning. The latter encompasses wisdom and understanding. These issues of strategic learning will be developed further in Chapter 6.

Organisational structures also strongly influence the learning of the leaders and the staff and children. If the majority of the time leaders and staff concentrate on operational and task issues and do not prioritise strategic and reflective discussions, then clearly little deep learning will take place. Organisational structures, such as splitting the strategic and operational functions into different meetings and different review cycles, emphasise the importance of the strategic dimension. Often, meetings have strategic issues tacked onto operational agendas. There should be a clear strategic meeting and review cycle in schools.

Systems in schools need to give attention to learning issues and strategic issues and not just to the urgency of operational demands if staff are to become reflective learners. One of the key leadership concepts is that leaders need first to look after themselves if they are then to look after the team and then the team can look after the organisation. The key to looking after oneself is to refresh oneself as a learner and to reflect on future directions and practice.

(iii) Strategic talent developers exert strategic influence. Strategic influence is based on how leaders gain commitment to the vision and direction of the school from those who work and learn in the organisation. If the school is not only to achieve improved outcomes and outputs but to do so in a sustainable way, then involving others and getting them on board is critical to its achievement. How can strategic leaders influence others to come on the strategic journey of the school? What follows are a number of factors that shape the leader's ability to influence others.

The first part of the influence-building process is to consider how people react to the leader and therefore the first stage is for the leader to look at his/her own leadership style and skills. Strategic leaders need to build trust with their colleagues and staff so others can believe in their motivations and their integrity. Important in this is how others perceive the leader and how effective she/he is at communicating those values and attributes. This credibility has two components: first, the credibility that comes from expertise and the ability to do the job; second, the credibility that comes from the character and integrity of the individual.

Strongly linked to this idea is the leader's own passion (Davies and Brighouse, 2008) for education and the role they can play in enhancing children's learning and life chances. Effective strategic leaders make opportunities to articulate their passion for education and to articulate what drives them to create a sense of moral purpose. Effective strategic leaders establish a credibility base grounded on doing what is best for the students and calling on all staff to make a difference through their interactions and role in the school. Moral leadership clearly needs to go beyond the rhetoric. The expression 'see something – do something about it' is a leadership value which needs to permeate the behaviour of all staff. The leader needs to create a moral purpose that translates ideals into action and is the initial catalyst of influence building.

Influencing others by involving them in the process is the starting place but there are a number of other significant factors. Clearly, building a foundation of understanding across the school is based on clear criteria for success but also on effective relationships so staff are involved in the process.

The purpose of this is to create a shared language and set of values so that the strategic leader connects to the 'heart' as well as the 'head'. The emotional commitment as well as the logical and rational commitment of staff is vital. However, in leading and managing staff it is important that strategic leaders are mindful of the organisational and political landscape. The importance of this section is that if the school is trying to recruit or develop leadership talent, then it needs a clear strategic framework in which to deploy that talent so that the people and the strategy are at one level aligned and at another level the individuals are empowered to deliver the strategy.

Reflection on strategy

1. List the four or five major strategic objectives that your school has agreed for the next 3–5 years.
2. Do all staff have a clear understanding of where the school is going and how they can contribute to that journey?
3. Do you have a clear idea of what talent you need to recruit and/or develop to enable the school to attain its strategic objectives?

Defining and developing values in school

Defining values is a process that must move beyond the rhetoric of statements on the school sign and on school websites to values that can be witnessed in terms of how leaders act and involve others in the school and wider community. Individuals most often judge a school by the people they meet in terms of the staff and the students. How these staff and students act and talk about their school and express pride in what they are doing, while working or studying there, is critical if values are to be transmitted in authentic and meaningful ways. Very often, we see new principals introduce an education which is 'values based' in rhetoric, something that is simply a slick package. It does not move beyond the paper to a deeper reality of sharing, concern and aspiration for all those involved in the school. Values can and should be challenging and be focused on what is best for all the students in the school community and the adults who nurture and guide them. Values should be seen in action.

Strategy can be considered to be what the school does, while values are more concerned with the how and why a school does what it does. Clearly, schools need a vision of what they are trying to do and how they are going to achieve it, and why that particular vision is important will articulate the school's values. It is important to embed the values of the school within a vision of its future. The importance of having a clear vision is seen by Nanus (1992: 16–18) who articulates the advantage of having a vision for the organisation:

➢ the right vision attracts commitment and energises people

➤ the right vision creates meaning in people's lives
➤ the right vision establishes a standard of excellence
➤ the right vision bridges the present and the future.

However, it is of little purpose if the vision is not translated into a value set which impacts on everyday actions and behaviours. One of the most inspiring and gifted educationalists is Terry Deal, and his book with Ken Peterson (1999: 26), *Shaping School Culture*, provides excellent definitions of values and beliefs:

> Values *are the conscious expressions of what an organisation stands for. Values define a standard of goodness, quality or excellence that undergirds behaviour and decision making, and what people care about. Values are not simply goals or outcomes; values are a deeper sense of what is important. Without an existing commitment, everything is relative; values focus attention and define success.*

> Beliefs *are how we comprehend and deal with the world around us. They are 'consciously held, cognitive views about truth and reality' (Ott, 1989: 39). Beliefs originate in group and personal experiences and through reading books and articles. Beliefs are powerful in schools because they represent the core understandings about student capacity (immutable or alterable), teacher responsibility for learning (little or lot), expert sources of teacher knowledge (experience, research or intuition), and educational success (will never happen or is achievable).*

It is important for schools to be able to define their values and also ensure that these values guide practice. We look at two examples of values, one from the business sector and one from the education sector.

Reckitt Benckiser Healthcare UK, a major international company, strives to create an organisational culture that is based on four cultural norms or values which are:

Insights from practice: Reckitt Benckiser values:

Entrepreneurship – 'We allow daring ideas to thrive'
Team Spirit – 'We work as one, united by common principles and attitudes'
Achievement – 'We don't just aim high, we always aim to outperform'
Ownership – 'We take the initiative to do what's needed'

Figure 2.2 *The four cultural norms or values for the Reckitt Benckiser organisation*

This example from Reckitt Benckiser provides a clear and unambiguous framework from which to recruit individuals that not only have the technical skills needed for different jobs but also share the core values system of the organisation. This core values system defines what generic 'talents' individuals need to bring to and develop within the company.

In the school sector, one of our research schools articulates its values as:

Insights from practice: a school example

Our central purpose is to provide quality learning experiences through a personalised pupil-centred education. In order to achieve this, we believe that the following values underpin all we do:

- the needs of the pupils come first
- everyone in our school community is special and important
- each of us works to improve on our previous bests
- learning is active, meaningful and creative
- we will have high expectations of ourselves and each other
- we work well in a stimulating learning environment.

At our school, we believe that every pupil will:

- be successful and confident
- be self-aware and co-operative
- have a continuing love of learning
- be independent and be able to work together
- be a solution finder
- be creative.

This value system defines what the school is trying to achieve. Once these values have been established, the school is able to frame the leadership values which develop from them. As well as values for the whole school, it is necessary for the individual leader to act with integrity. This involves the leader looking at their own leadership values and how the leadership talent they seek to develop can share those values.

Values and beliefs and the leader

Building a set of values and beliefs in an organisation will be successful only if the leader is perceived to be acting within a moral framework.

Kouzes and Posner (1999: 49) argue that 'human beings don't put their hearts into something they don't believe in'. Their research into values puts forward the view that it is the clarity of an individual's values that makes a difference to their level of commitment to the organisation. Where these coincide with the clarity of organisational values, then there is the highest level of commitment. Interestingly, where there were high levels of clarity of personal values but some confusion over organisational values, there were still high levels of commitment, but where clarity of organisational values was not supported by high levels of personal values then commitment was limited. What values or moral characteristics do leaders need to establish the moral culture of the organisation?

Brubaker and Colbe (2005: 176–81) in discussing the components of the moral culture draw on research by Josephson (1990) to outline core values that respondents found desirable in ethical leaders. We will outline each of them in turn.

- Honesty – that colleagues can rely on what you say is the truth.
- Integrity – words and actions are aligned.
- Promise keeping – the ability to deliver on what you agree to do.
- Loyalty – to the organisation you work for and the people who you work with.
- Fairness – you have the same set of expectations from all staff.
- Concern for others – in their working and personal lives.
- Respect for others – respecting their individual differences and diversity.
- Law abiding – operating within the accountability and regulatory frameworks.
- Pursuit of excellence – striving for high achievements by all staff and students.
- Personal accountability – take responsibility, admit mistakes and share success.

The significance of this is that schools need both to define their organisational values and their leadership values. Most importantly, it is necessary to both articulate them clearly and also ensure, through training and the culture of the school, that the values are lived and practised. In terms of talent management, this then enables the school to recruit and develop individuals into the value system of the school. The following exercises are useful tools for the reader to reflect on practice in their own school.

Reflection on values

➤ List the key values that your school stands for.
➤ How often do you reinforce the values in formal or informal situations?
➤ Does your leadership team discuss the values that underpin the way it operates and interacts with others within the school and wider community?
➤ Do you share those key values?

How values affect leadership styles is demonstrated in the following leadership examples.

Insights from practice: values in action – one school, three leaders

This is a case study undertaken over a 12-year period at one school in England where one leader 'Peter' served as head teacher for three years, he was succeeded by 'Jane' for six years, Pat took over when Jane retired.

Peter as leader

It is clear that for Peter, targets and SATs results are all-important and he continually forces teachers to adopt shallow learning approaches to enable children to replicate facts in official government tests. He is a very articulate individual and good at promoting himself. He was very successful in persuading the last Ofsted inspection team that the school's test results were a good measure of how good the school was. Staff, while appreciating the importance of the testing regime, are increasingly demoralised by the approaches being advocated by Peter. Achievements are hyped up, especially of the boys' football team where the 'few' team members are singled out for praise whilst the 'many' (including all the girls) receive little attention. Marketing is based on test results and achievements in sport which are both good. Peter is especially good at promoting himself at large publicity meetings but rarely attends the reporting to parents' evenings. In terms of leadership as outlined by Collins (2001), this would equate to level 3 or 4 leadership where the 'I' of leadership is paramount; everything is seen in terms of how it affects the individual leader.

(Continues)

(Continued)

There are alternative cultures being set up in the school by teachers who seek to protect themselves. One such culture is seen in which staff undertake a number of compliance activities that fulfil the requirements of the head teacher. The other is where they work among themselves in small groups to build learning and teaching cultures that they are confident with and they believe promote 'deep learning' for pupils. The staff feel things are 'done to them' and often feel 'done in' (Novak, 2009) and are increasingly withdrawing into their own classrooms. There is an increasing compliance with the wishes of Peter rather than of a broader professional debate. There is little articulation of the values of the school and of the ethical basis on which individuals relate to each other. Planning is short-term, run by the head teacher alone and focused on one-year targets. Peter writes a one-year school development plan by himself. He has also written the school policies copied from websites. There is no policy for learning. Peter is involved in educational consultancy and has a reputation for not always being in the school. He is not involved in classrooms and does little in the way of mentoring or coaching staff. Some teachers have involved their trade union in complaints against the head teacher. Governors are increasingly at 'loggerheads' with Peter and relationships have deteriorated considerably. However, through the external inspection system, the school is judged to be successful. The values that underpin leadership are sadly lacking and both the staff and the parents don't trust Peter.

Jane as leader

Jane took over the school after considerable previous experience in headship. While recognising the need to deliver short-term results, she believes far more in developing meaningful learning through an integrated curricular approach with highly engaged staff. With a clear personal and professional educational value system, she possesses a quiet determination but is not a natural 'marketer' and does not 'sell' herself at the expense of the staff team or the school. She believes in distributed leadership and seeks to build a learning community of staff and pupils. In terms of Collins' levels of leadership, she could be categorised as a level 5 leader – seeking success for the school and not personalised success for herself. In a sense, this could be characterised as quiet leadership.

By refocusing the school on learning and adopting different learning approaches, she aims to meet short-term targets through the quality of the children's experience being reflected in their achievements and those demonstrated in the outcome measures. These targets are achieved by reculturing the staff into a high achievement culture which focuses on the individual child's learning needs. Her philosophy is one of working with the staff so that the culture is one of 'done with' rather than 'done to'. She sets out a way of working together based on honesty and integrity as well as transparency as a means of building a professional dialogue within the school.

Although clearly a people person, Jane's main challenge has been to break the school out of a culture of complacency and move it to one of high achievement by challenging performance to achieve excellence. This change has involved a slow process of building professional accountability for children's learning and challenging previous assumptions and attitudes to learning. She has a clear strategic vision for the school and has both the patience and the determination to achieve it. She sees the staff as a totality and teaching, teacher support and administrative staff are all part of the same team, which is a value that underpins the whole culture.

Compared with Peter, she is far more in evidence in the classroom, working with teachers, monitoring standards and involving the leadership team in taking greater responsibilities for colleagues' teaching and learning approaches. She is particularly committed to developing strategic and future plans to run alongside the mandatory short-term school improvement plan. Jane clearly lives the values which the school holds.

Pat as leader

Pat joined the school when it was judged to be 'good with outstanding attributes'. But Pat didn't care about the history of the school, nor did he care about the culture of the school he was joining – he did not take time to reflect on the core values of the school and the way people worked very effectively together. Pat did not want to understand the school through the eyes of the talented staff. The overriding motivation for Pat was to prove himself, at the expense of whoever else. This head teacher is a good example of someone shouting about the rhetoric of values without it affecting the reality of his practice. Pat is unable to recognise the good practice in school and the well-established approach to children's behaviour and learning. On take-up of the post, he immediately introduced a new 'bought in' commercial values approach

(Continues)

(Continued)

to the curriculum and made a big issue of it outside the school without working with his colleagues for an effective introduction. The approach is articulated through slogans and window dressing but sadly the reality in the school is somewhat different – a school which had values at the heart of its practice is now valueless. For example, on his first staff development day, Pat sent the learning assistants away to 'get the classrooms ready' while he did 'important' work just with the teaching staff. This sent powerful signals to all staff about support staff not being valued or respected. It was announced that all staff would have the opportunity to talk with him in a professional review. In reality, this was only offered to teaching staff and took the form of an interview rather than the professional dialogue that all staff had previously found motivating and worthwhile. After a year in post, Pat has not observed colleagues in classrooms and does not work alongside them but leads through sending numerous e-mails from his office. Staff have to make appointments to see him which are often in two or three weeks' time and there is no response to the day-to-day challenges that staff need to share with him. The interests of the children are no longer put first, previously a core value in action. Staff are beginning to work individually and in isolation, something supported by Pat as he is removing all opportunities for joint planning and shared learning. All well-established processes, such as performance review and professional learning, are thrown out, but nothing is put in place to replace them. Staff are increasingly demoralised, demotivated and lack trust in the leadership of the head teacher who they believe is only 'out for himself'. The latest Ofsted report reflects the deterioration in the effectiveness of the school, judging it to be barely satisfactory. The talented deputy head is also demoralised, and following the head teacher's derogatory comments about him in the inspection report he too does not trust the head and is frightened to initiate change. It is a clear case of actions by the head teacher which 'do to' staff so they feel 'done in'. A values-based approach to everything in school, not just the curriculum, has to be lived through the interactions between people in the school, through care, honesty, respect and trust. The failure of this leader to show any value through his actions, and his failure to acknowledge collective responsibility but instead to focus on his individual glory, demonstrates the failure to promote any values in action.

Implications of the leadership examples

While the names of the leaders have been changed, the reality of the examples demonstrates the significance of building longer-term strategic capacity in schools. In terms of Collins' (2001) dimensions of professional will and personal humility, it is clear that one head, Jane, is far more likely to reflect these and put the school on to a successful path that is values-led. Also significant is the people dimension of Jane's leadership style with the involvement of colleagues and building the capacity to work together through sustainable relationships.

Making judgements about which leader is successful needs to focus on the questions of whose leadership is sustainable and strategic and which leadership is based on deep-seated educational and moral values. Judging failure is framed by a lack of moral compass.

Unless schools can empower and motivate those who work within it with a sense of moral purpose and attainable achievements, the school will simply move from one set of operational targets to another without building a true learning community. Our argument is that before schools and individuals can start thinking about developing a talent-management approach, the core question of 'talent for what?' needs to be answered. In this context, the strategic vision of the school and its value system needs to underpin all its actions.

So our staged approach to talent management is as follows:

1. Define values and strategy.
2. Establish rigorous performance evaluation.
3. Performance management – define and evaluate performance or potential.
4. Develop talent.
5. Establish powerful professional learning.
6. The architecture to support talent development.
7. Create a talent-management culture.
8. Develop school and system talent.
9. Integrate talent management into whole-school processes.

All the other stages depend on the first one being in place before the school can develop its approach. To assess where the reader is in terms of their own organisation, each chapter will have a self-reflection exercise based on the four elements of our leadership model: values, personal qualities, working with others and strategic acumen.

Conclusion

This chapter has emphasised that schools clearly need to establish values and strategies as a basis for developing a talent-management approach. The chapter considers that talent management cannot be a bolt-on event, rather it has to be integrated into a staged process. This process should be underpinned by the values held by the leaders, shared and lived by the whole school and reflected in the strategic framework articulated by the school.

Suggested further reading

Davies, B. (2011) *Leading the Strategically Focused School*. London: Sage.

Davies, B. and Davies, B.J. (2009) 'Strategic leadership', in B. Davies (ed.) *Essentials of School Leadership*. London: Sage.

Davies, B. and Brighouse, T. (2008) *Passionate Leadership*. London: Sage.

Deal, T. and Peterson, K.D. (1999) *Shaping School Culture*. San Francisco, CA: Jossey-Bass.

Talent assessment framework: where are you now? Strategy and values

Rate yourself (in partnership discussion) on the following categories.

1 = not at all; 2 = only partially; 3 = to a degree; 4 = very often; 5 = completely

Values

Are values clearly articulated for the school?	1	2	3	4	5
Do your personal values align with those of the school?	1	2	3	4	5
Are values part of the language and actions of the school?	1	2	3	4	5

Personal qualities

Leaders have the confidence to articulate strategic vision.	1	2	3	4	5
Leaders take considered risks to achieve objectives.	1	2	3	4	5
Leaders learn from experience.	1	2	3	4	5

Working with others

Leaders communicate clear strategy and vision.	1	2	3	4	5
Are leaders credible to others in their roles?	1	2	3	4	5
Do leaders both challenge and support colleagues?	1	2	3	4	5

Strategic acumen

Are leaders able to see the 'big picture'?	1	2	3	4	5
Does the school have a clearly defined strategy?	1	2	3	4	5
Is there intent to identify and develop talent?	1	2	3	4	5

Those items you have rated '1' or '2' would need to be developed while those ranked '4' or '5' need to be celebrated and sustained. Those rated '3' warrant further reflection.

Talent Identification

Chapter 3

Performance evaluation

This chapter considers:

- ➤ linking performance management with whole-school processes
- ➤ approaches for developing leadership potential
- ➤ defining performance standards and the importance of trust
- ➤ the role of challenge and support
- ➤ identifying talent for leadership
- ➤ motivating staff for leadership.

Key ideas

Knowing how to identify, develop and get the best out of people is vital for any organisation. How to identify people who are doing a great job in their present role and how to help them to develop their potential is a vital process for the management of talent. Performance is the result of behaviour, how you choose to act and what you choose to say. We demonstrate who we are through our chosen behaviours. Behaviour is observable, detectable and learnable. Each role in school has an identifiable set of behaviours, setting out how to undertake the role, which will create the best performance. If we start by articulating and defining these behaviours, we can be explicit about our expectations for each role. This should not be a list detailing the 'what' of the job, often found in traditional job descriptions, but rather an explanation of the specific behaviours expected to ensure high-level performance in that role and which are aligned to the value system of the organisation. This is the 'how' of the job. Performance is job-specific, and good performance is when behaviour matches the expectations for that role or post. If we are to enable people to be the best they can be, we need to identify the specific key behaviours for each post.

A renewed era of accountability began in the 1980s, when statutory procedures replaced voluntary systems of professionalism. Since then it has been statutory that every governing body has a policy outlining the performance-management process for their school. Revised regulations came into force in 2007 and amendments occur periodically, for example the involvement of the performance-management process in 'threshold' assessments in 2009. Model performance-management policies are readily available, which now also set out classroom observation protocols and the timing of the performance management annual cycle. Everyone accepts that performance management happens and schools ensure that all teachers take part. But is the performance-management process part of the broader culture of the school? Does it just happen or is it an integrated process for school improvement? In our research, we have talked with many groups about talent management and often the response is 'Oh yes, we do that.' Our challenge to readers is, do you just 'do that', which is a superficial agreement, or do you ensure that the process of performance management matters? Underperformance of staff probably presents the hardest challenge for educational leaders. Staff are the most costly resource in a school and are central to school improvement processes, therefore all performance should be evaluated, and there should be a consequence from the evaluation where performance is celebrated and supported or challenged and supported to become more effective. Evaluation of performance, and subsequent actions, really matter.

Reflection point

Does your performance-management process:
➤ encourage self-reflection?
➤ align objectives across teams?
➤ improve motivation and morale?
➤ make actions clear and transparent?
➤ ask people what they need to do to make a difference?
➤ identify and develop talent?

It is easy to say 'yes' but how do you know that your process matters to staff and makes a difference? In many schools, performance management is a process where participants go through the motions; it does not seriously affect any of these outcomes. To all those people who say 'yes, we do that', we ask whether you have evaluated the process from the participants' point of view? Have you effected any improvements since introducing your process?

The key success criteria for the performance-management process is whether participants are trained for and regularly take part in an honest and trustworthy review. Is the performance-management process improved through acting on the experiences of the reviewed and reviewers? The Rewards and Incentive Group (RIG) framed a view of a new 'professionalism' in the 1998 Green Paper *Teachers: Meeting the Challenge of Change*. This recognised how important it is for teachers to maintain and improve their professional practice. It promoted professional development as an integral part of everyday professional life. It is easy to accept that if all staff focus on their practice and develop their expertise, then they will be better able to improve children's learning and have improved job satisfaction and progression. It is obvious that schools need to ensure that their arrangements for performance management are managed effectively, transparently and fairly. But does the performance-management process matter to all staff?

Enhancing the performance of all staff

Establishing a clear focus for professional learning is an essential element of any review of performance. Everyone should consider how they can improve their professional practice and how they will be supported. We have to accept that not everyone will want to take the opportunity to become the best they can be or to reach their potential. Outside circumstances, personal circumstances or even the lack of self-will stop some people becoming the best they can be – to be talented takes work! All staff should have the opportunity to develop their abilities and explore their potential abilities. How people deal with opportunities is an important aspect of talent identification.

Reflection point

Does your school have:

➤ a culture where all staff feel confident and empowered to participate and gain from the performance-management process?
➤ a process where the professional dialogue is ongoing, positive and has an impact?
➤ an environment where everyone is engaged in professional learning?
➤ an integrated system where performance management is linked with the school evaluation, school-improvement planning and professional-learning processes?

> ➤ a system for all staff to review the process?
> ➤ an approach that enables all staff, both reviewer and reviewed, to take part in skill training to include self-evaluation, active listening, conflict resolution and giving and receiving feedback?
> ➤ a system where those who manage staff, including head teachers, engage in a professional dialogue with them, respect them as professionals, make decisions about their work and contribute fairly and openly?
> ➤ moderate reviews and opportunities across school?

Professional standards provide the underpinning to discussions about performance. Standards for teaching staff which define the professional attributes, understanding, knowledge and skills for different stages in a career are readily available. Some schools have adopted or created similar standards for support staff. Support staff account for the majority of most school staffing provision and it is important that all staff have the same access to performance review and professional-learning opportunities and have the opportunity to become excellent in their role. It is important that the process also informs the talent-management process, therefore standards for talent identification and potential could be used for self-evaluation and career review. Schools should have an agreed process for the expected standards for leadership in their school for all staff and develop a culture of transparency, fairness and consistency where all staff are supported throughout their careers, engaged in effective professional learning and are able to contribute to improvements for pupils. Staff with the potential to become excellent leaders will need to develop the skills of observation. One school supported this through a series of coached observations over a series of lessons in the year, as detailed in Figure 3.1.

How to develop a system where performance management is linked with the school evaluation, school-improvement planning and professional-learning processes

One of the advantages of linking the processes of performance management, school evaluation, school-improvement planning and professional learning is to reduce workload, but more importantly using data to inform other processes is vital. To align objectives with a

GUIDELINES FOR PAIRED OBSERVATION FOR PROFESSIONAL LEARNING		
	Experienced observer (EO)	**Learner observer (LO)**
Lesson observation 1	• Observe • Record • Discuss with learner observer • Lead feedback • Discuss with learner observer	• Written record for discussion to be destroyed • Discuss observation and feedback • Observe feedback • Discuss with EO
Lesson observation 2	• Make written record for discussion (to be destroyed if agreement) • Discuss observation and feedback • Feedback if not LO • Discuss with LO	• Observe • Record • Discuss observation and feedback with EO • Lead feedback (alone) if EO agrees • Discuss with EO
Lesson observation 2	• Make written record for discussion (to be destroyed if agreement) • Discuss observation and feedback • Observe feedback • Discuss with LO	• Observe • Record • Discuss with EO • Lead feedback (observed by EO) • Discuss with EO
Lesson observation 4	• No part in process if appropriate • Discuss with LO	• Lead observation if appropriate • Discuss process with EO

Figure 3.1 *Guidelines for paired observation for professional learning*

focus on learning and teaching is common sense. Through highlighting priorities, the school self-evaluation and strategic improvement planning processes help to influence and inform objective setting for staff. The priorities can be translated into professional-learning opportunities. How do we do this? We need to ensure that policies and procedures are reviewed so they are consistent with each other; most schools will make sure that performance and pay policies are coherent and that these processes are logical and match in timescales. But does the cycle of school-improvement planning fit with the cycle of school self-evaluation to ensure information effects practice? Is the cycle of professional learning determined by the school's strategy, performance management and self-evaluation activities? Do the school-improvement plan and self-evaluation inform the performance-management process?

It is important that the development and implementation of the performance-management process is seen as a whole-school process. Everyone should be engaged in the process and feel ownership of it. The process should be integrated into a coherent framework and not be seen as an 'add-on'. Performance management:

> should be a process that is part of the school culture and not an annual form-filling event
> should be used to enable an understanding of what the school is trying to achieve and how it can improve
> should encourage high self-expectations, self-reflection and evaluation in order to support personal improvement
> should enable staff to share in the success of the organisation, with their contribution celebrated
> should be a core process in the approach to school improvement and talent management.

How do we use this integrated processes approach to develop leadership potential?

As we have discussed earlier, enabling people to progress their leadership development by supporting their ability to reflect on situations, to think about what went well and what could be developed further are elements of effective performance management and enable the identification of leadership potential. Reflection should become a natural activity – looking at what we do and considering the effect of our behaviours in terms of processes as well as people should be important development activities. It is important to ask the following two questions as highlighted.

Reflection point

> What is the impact of the performance-management process on the identification and development of talented staff?
> How do you know?

The performance-management process should enable a balance between professional development and organisational development. By creating a framework for coaching and individualised development, we mirror in the environment for adult learning that learning environment we create for pupil learning. For talent management, there should be regular planned opportunities for review.

Defining standards understood by all

A starting point for any performance process must be clarity about roles, not least in the process for the identification of talent. We should ask:

> ➤ What are the key accountabilities for each role?
> ➤ What professional skills, knowledge and attitudes are required to deliver those accountabilities?
> ➤ What professional characteristics are required?

If performance standards are clear for everyone, it is easier to conduct self-review and colleague reviews. Like most processes introduced through the accountability era, it is difficult to accept that the performance-management process can both meet accountability and development needs. Therefore, it is important to establish aims for the performance-management system. We see the aims in terms of accountability and development as follows:

Evaluation for accountability

> ➤ To identify levels of staff performance.
> ➤ To ensure staff have clarity about their current level of performance.

Evaluation for development

> ➤ To coach staff to support:
>   ➤ performance improvement
>   ➤ development of future potential.
> ➤ To develop commitment to the organisation through discussion of career progression, aspirations and opportunities.
> ➤ To recognise achievements and motivate staff.

Enabling honest conversations: the importance of trust

The quality of the relationship between the reviewer and reviewee is critical in the performance-management process. However technically correct a process is, without trust there will be little effective feedback and coaching. Trust is an expectation about the actions of others. You can have confidence in the process of performance management but trust in the people to tell the truth is necessary for the process to have any impact. Jones et al. (2006: 89) identify 'trust builders' which include:

➤ clarity of communication, both oral and written
➤ establishing clear and positive expectations
➤ listening actively and attending to what others say
➤ openness to explore new possibilities
➤ admitting mistakes
➤ valuing, respecting views, ideas and ideals of others
➤ making and keeping commitments
➤ sensitivity, being straightforward and honest.

Trust is involuntary – you can't make yourself trust but you can act in ways that help trust develop. The 'trust builders' are actions which support someone acting in another's interests – they nurture trust. Staff may cooperate in the process without trust, but trust sustains effective interactions and enhances the quality of the cooperation. Trust is a two-way process and the 'trust builders' should be two-way too. Trust is directly linked with truthfulness and must come from within in order to be a central value for the school community. Similarly, an effective performance-management process should be accountability from within, a meaningful evaluation process which enables personal development and fulfilment. In many schools, it is just a statutory process, which is conducted in order to meet accountability from external sources. Performance-management processes for external rather than intrinsic motivations will never support the nurturing of talent. The process as well as the judgements must be truthful in order to add value to staff and school. Leaders must act in trustworthy ways and communicate honestly.

Regular informed discussions about the quality of teaching or performance in a leadership role is vital. A calendar of lesson observations enables staff to be observed with a planned different focus each time over a three-year cycle. The leadership team is then able to analyse the main issues and strengths for an individual and for the school. Having critical professional discussions about teaching quality and strategy is an indication of an improving school. An approach which expects leaders to analyse the themes which emerge from lesson observations and feed these into operational plans and plans for professional learning is an effective way to link the processes. Leaders should also use the identified behaviours for leadership roles in order to discuss and identify potential talent.

Challenge and support

It is well established that recognition enhances motivation and is linked to the core values of respect and trust in our leadership development model. This is the main reason why the performance-evaluation process should be based on continuing feedback through the year, and why it should be an ongoing professional dialogue. What a difference it would make if reviewers in the performance-management process had their performance of the skill of recognising people's achievements identified as a target in their own appraisal! How do we create a culture where we challenge colleagues professionally and yet are comfortable enough to motivate them to want to do more?

Some people find the process of performance management positive and motivating, where success is recognised and celebrated and where guidance and opportunities support further development. For others, the process is demoralising and daunting. In talking with staff who exemplify these different positions, the variation in view could be explained in terms of trust – for the first set of people, trust and confidence in themselves and their ability and for the second set of people, a lack of trust and confidence in the reviewer and the school process.

Like most processes and systems in school, the importance of relationships is at the core of an effective school. The best systems support and challenge the way we work. If performance management is to be a key change process, then it has to balance support and challenge.

360-degree feedback

Self-review is a very powerful tool – learning and development only happen when a person accepts that learning is necessary for improvement. However, self-review may not represent the total view of a situation since the perception or judgements are one-sided. Frameworks which clarify the behaviours expected from each role could be

LIBRARY, UNIVERSITY OF CHESTER

used to gain feedback from different perspectives. Any performance management process should, we believe, continue throughout the year and be focused on dialogue and feedback. One of the tools which meets these elements and which is taken from the business world is 360-degree feedback. This process involves the reviewee's colleagues in sharing their views of the person's performance. This gives a more complete picture of performance, since different people may see the person in a range of different circumstances and contexts. The following insight from practice describes one school's use of this approach when evaluating the performance of potential leadership talent.

Insight from practice

Performance is generally deemed measurable, quantifiable and talent, for me, does not necessarily have just quantifiable boundaries. This is also why some aspects of annual performance review and target setting in schools fail to explore the less measurable aspects of performance or even promote talent to flourish through being too constricting and constraining. All too often, schools are concerned with tick boxes and bureaucracy, driven by government and fuelled by unions and, in being so, miss opportunities to really fly.

In addition to a more formal process of performance target setting which outlines measurable targets such as learner outcomes, customer service performance and professional development needs, my school also uses a talent competencies review spreadsheet (designed by one of my vice principals as part of an MBA assignment) in which colleagues are asked to anonymously score their colleagues in the six areas of:

➢ leadership
➢ results orientation
➢ interpersonal skills
➢ personal organisation
➢ innovation
➢ learning.

Although not in any sense claiming to be an exact science, the discussion of responses from four or more colleagues on aspects of an individual's performance in this respect does serve as a useful way to raise their awareness of the way they perform and of their particular elements and areas of strength as identified by some of their colleagues. More importantly, it gets people talking about what they can do and what they need to do in terms of identifying leadership potential.

Just because an individual stands out as a leader in one area does not necessarily mean that they have the talent to juggle the balls needed to lead in the wider arena. The really talented leader for me is always the one who knows when their talent is best used but that they do not necessarily have to be the leader up front. These are the individuals who have the emotional intelligence to understand the objectives, the strategies and the need to perform to get the results. Their ego and drive is channelled into the creativity and innovation of the task not in the controlling of it. Their direction setting is clear and intelligent and their contribution thoughtful and reflective throughout. It is this talent and willingness to engage in discussion about it that steers towards high-performing individuals and, ultimately, our leaders of the future.

Research suggests, and the practice insight above supports this, that successful 360-degree feedback requires:

➤ a culture focused on trust and truth
➤ a clear strategic framework
➤ leadership support and involvement
➤ the sensitivity and willingness to discuss any issue
➤ an organisation-wide willingness to change and improve.

The identification of talent for leadership

During our research, many leaders said to us 'we recognise talent when we see it' or 'we just know, it's a gut reaction'. However, we believe that talent identification shouldn't be left to this 'chance' arrangement of being spotted by 'gut reaction'. Could it be that there isn't a deficit of talent in the system, but just inadequate ways of identification and development? The starting point has to be the job itself. We have already suggested that the best possible performance for each job can be described through a set of specific behaviours. Once these are defined, they can be used by the member of staff to determine (a) if they can do them and (b) if they want to do them, and through a performance management process by others to evaluate if, in their opinion, the person can do the role effectively. What could these behaviours look like? The following are examples of behaviours in specific roles using our model:

School business manager

Values	Work within a strong code of ethics and practice
Strategic acumen	Evaluate the future implications of decisions
	Develop integrated processes
Working with people	Enable people to focus on how they can make their best contribution
	Develop a network of contacts
Personal qualities	Generate enthusiasm

Middle leader

Values	Always focus on the best interests of the children
Strategic acumen	Build on the team's ideas and initiatives for change
Working with others	Enable people to identify and build on best practice
	Give team members frequent feedback
Personal qualities	Be persistent in the face of difficulties to find solutions
	Encourage self-motivation to inspire others to be at their best

In order to identify and develop potential leaders, it is important to be clear about what behaviours are needed for the leadership role and then to give the person the opportunity to demonstrate what the job requires, while providing support throughout the learning process.

Reflection point

➤ When your school leadership team discusses job roles and future roles, how much time do you give to the 'what?' key performance indicators and targets and how much time on the 'how' behaviours?

➤ Who is in a role which needs different behaviours to their present performance? How will you support them?

➤ Do your job descriptions define areas of responsibility or tasks to be led and managed?

Motivation

We have identified self-motivation as a key factor in the model of leadership for the future and therefore a potential leader should demonstrate this characteristic. Bruce and Pepitone (1999: ix) suggest that it is important 'to create a truly motivational organisation, one that inspires each employee to do their best every day especially when the manager isn't looking'.

We each choose our behaviour and the only person who can change your behaviour is you. A person is motivated to do what they perceive to be in their own best interests. A leader cannot motivate another person but they can influence what they may be motivated to do. No one can cause a motivation but leaders and team members and the task can influence the response. Leaders can create a climate which is motivational. Motivation is intrinsic but can be affected by extrinsic aspects. Our motivation determines the degree of engagement and governs our choice of behaviour.

Evans (2003) found that teacher morale and motivation are influenced less by externally initiated factors, such as salary or conditions of service, than by factors coming from the context of work. Leadership and staff relationships emerge as key influencing factors. Maslow's hierarchy of needs (Maslow, 1954) is one of the best-known and influential theories on motivation. It is founded on the idea that goals or needs underpin motivation and that these needs are all driven by self not the environment or other people. The basic physiological needs are related to survival, the need for security and safety (see Figure 3.2). Maslow's theory then addresses the ego needs where self-esteem and recognition motivate human behaviour. The highest order need is seen as self-actualisation, where the need to recognise our personal potential and become all we can become is the motivator.

Other theorists have criticised the incremental hierarchy of the theory that low-level needs should be satisfied before the higher-order needs can be met. While Maslow's ideas are often represented as a hierarchical pyramid in management books, this doesn't seem to have been originated by him. More recent theorists suggest that the pyramid should be inverted to demonstrate that the greatest needs are in the esteem and self-actualisation range. Even given this debate, it is important that the underlying attitudes and behaviours described, whether developed or satisfied sequentially or in parallel, are important to our consideration of potential leaders.

The key components of these needs can be seen in the following:

Physical needs	Social needs	Esteem	Self-actualisation
➤ Safety	➤ Respect for others	➤ Recognition	➤ Recognition of
➤ Survival	➤ Belonging	➤ Self-fulfilment	personal potential
			➤ Becoming all we can become

Figure 3.2 *Motivational needs*

The importance of the model, when thinking of talented staff, is that aspirant leaders must have self-belief, but more importantly they must be motivated by the higher-order needs of achievement. Staff may be capable of undertaking leadership roles but without the need to achieve, the self-motivation, that capability will not be realised. People with potential leadership talent need to be motivated and then need the opportunity to develop leadership role mastery.

How is motivation effected by external conditions? Some people are motivated by more pay, which satisfies a lower-order need and when received motivation may stop, so this motivation does not move anyone beyond the minimum effort needed to achieve the reward. If staff members are motivated by being able to make decisions (esteem) or understand how they add value to the organisation (actualisation), the way they perceive their work is changed and their belief in their own capability is enhanced and they have greater meaning to their work. The higher the need satisfied by their work, the greater the motivation will be. Needs will change over time and according to context of the situation but understanding the theory can guide our identification of leadership potential. Maslow saw 'individual need' as the only motivator – we see this as true, in that no one else can motivate you, however we believe that leaders, others and the job contribute to the individual response. Adair (1990: 41) highlights the significance of leaders recognising the importance of the motivation of others:

> *the idea that leaders are born and not made is half truth. The full truth is that they are (about) half born and (more or less) half made – by experience and thought and training and teaching by others ... paradoxically it takes a long time to become a natural leader.*

So what moves us to action comes from within but can be influenced from without, by others. How can we support the needs which help talented individuals develop?

Esteem needs

- ➤ regular feedback
- ➤ the ability to demonstrate talents
- ➤ involvement in the strategic-planning process
- ➤ appreciation and respect.

Self-actualisation

- ➤ autonomy in projects
- ➤ the freedom to be creative
- ➤ mistakes being seen as learning experiences
- ➤ opportunities for greater challenge.

A useful perspective is provided by Dweck: 'The hallmark of successful individuals is that they love learning, seek challenges, value effort and persist in the face of difficulties' (Dweck, 2000: 1). Dweck describes these attributes as 'mastery-oriented qualities', where individuals remain focused on achieving mastery in spite of difficulties. Potential leaders will display this mastery response to problem solving and change. Dweck's research suggests that people with 'mastery qualities' do not question their ability in challenging situations but see 'failure' as opportunities for learning and development; so too with potential leaders, these situations do not cause them to give up, rather they become more motivated to achieve and give more effort. They will have learnt that confidence through success of an event is not as important as the confidence to know that you have the ability to learn in different situations.

Can we measure or motivate potential?

We can evaluate what someone can do now in their present role through an effective performance-management process and we can use this to attempt to predict what they may be capable of in the future. Other factors such as how motivated a person is will support the identification of potential leaders. What can we do to prioritise the support of motivation of others? First, you need to be inspired yourself – competent enthusiasm inspires, especially if it is combined with the key value of trust. It is impossible to motivate those who are not self-motivated, therefore it makes sense to select those who are. Persistence and perseverance are key personal qualities which evidence motivation.

Conclusion

In this chapter, we have attempted to move the debate away from a 'tick list' approach of performance management by engaging our reader in a more fundamental review of performance evaluation. This requires an understanding of the role of performance evaluation as an identifying and motivating process. As such, it should be linked into whole-school improvement strategies and approaches. The key factor in moving performance management from a compliant legal framework approach to the reality of a deep-rooted school improvement approach is trust. Personal trust and organisational trust are often neglected when considering leadership and need renewed attention.

Suggested further reading

Bruce, A. and Pepitone, J.S. (1999) *Motivating Employees.* New York: McGraw Hill.

Dweck, C.S. (2000) *Self-theories: Their Role in Motivation, Personality and Development.* Philadelphia, PA: Psychology Press.

Jones, J., Jenkin, M. and Lord, S. (2006) *Developing Effective Teacher Performance.* London: PCP.

To assess where the reader is in terms of their own organisation, the following self-reflection exercise is based on the four elements of our leadership model: values, personal qualities, working with others and strategic acumen.

Talent assessment framework: where are you now? Performance evaluation

Rate yourself (in partnership discussion) on the following categories.

1 = not at all; 2 = only partially; 3 = to a degree; 4 = very often; 5 = completely

Values

Does your practice demonstrate that all staff are valued?	1 2 3 4 5
Do staff trust the integrity of the evaluation process?	1 2 3 4 5
Can staff have honest conversations about performance?	1 2 3 4 5

Personal qualities

Do you undertake honest self-evaluations?	1 2 3 4 5
Are you self-motivated to improve?	1 2 3 4 5
Are you able to receive honest feedback constructively?	1 2 3 4 5

Working with others

Can you both challenge and support others?	1 2 3 4 5
How well do you communicate effectiveness to others?	1 2 3 4 5
Do you recognise and communicate others' achievements?	1 2 3 4 5

Strategic acumen

Do you have a staff plan for now and for the future?	1 2 3 4 5
Is staff evaluation linked with strategic processes?	1 2 3 4 5
Have you identified future talent in your organisation?	1 2 3 4 5

Those items you have rated '1' or '2' would need to be developed while those ranked '4' or '5' need to be celebrated and sustained. Those rated '3' warrant further reflection.

Chapter 4

Performance or potential?

This chapter considers:

- ➤ why leadership potential is important
- ➤ that performance is not the same as potential
- ➤ talent identification
- ➤ the *Rush to the Top* research (Hay Group, 2008)
- ➤ the identification and match of performance and potential
- ➤ lessons from practice.

Key ideas

'Performance' is the ability to do the job a person has now. 'Potential' is the capability to do a particular new and different job in the future. Many things may stop a top performer from being a successful leader, not least their own desire and motivation. The first step in assessing leadership potential may therefore be to find out who wants to move into leadership. However, while the desire for headship or school leadership is important, it is only a first step. From a system or school point of view, the real challenge is to identify those individuals with outstanding leadership potential and provide them with a coherent pathway for their development. Talent-management processes which nominate staff without their knowledge by relying on the opinion of others will fail to build a realistic and credible partnership with the individuals involved. Ensuring that resources and effort are given to people who want to advance is as important as their ability to advance. We have established that the performance-management process must be open and honest and involve the opinions of the member of staff. Staff must demonstrate that they are motivated to seek professional advancement and therefore will be committed and interested in any changes needed. This involves both current and future dialogues with staff as can be seen in the following insight from practice.

> **Insight from practice**
>
> One school in the east Midlands offers all their staff a professional review with a member of the school leadership team. This encourages a discussion of:
>
> ➤ What would you like to be doing in five years' time?
> ➤ What do you need to do to get there?
> ➤ What does this look like for two and for four years' time?

Why is leadership potential important?

One of the most significant pieces of research on school leadership investigated the impact of leadership on the core purpose of schools, that of student learning as measured by student performance. This was the *Seven Strong Claims about Successful School Leadership* research by Leithwood et al. (2006). The research highlighted the significance of school leadership and in our view the critical importance of developing future leadership. These claims were:

1. School leadership is second only to classroom teaching as an influence on pupil learning.
2. Almost all successful leaders draw on the same repertoire of basic leadership practices.
3. The ways in which leaders apply these basic leadership practices, not the practices themselves, demonstrate responsiveness to (rather than dictation by) the contexts in which they work.
4. School leaders improve teaching and learning indirectly and most powerfully through their influence on staff motivation, commitment and working conditions.
5. School leadership has a greater influence on schools and students when it is widely distributed.
6. Some patterns of the distribution of leadership are more effective than others.
7. A small handful of personal traits explain a high proportion of the variation in leadership effectiveness.

If we are to continue the transformation of learning and improve the life chances of children, then effective leadership which will impact on student performance is critical. Identifying and developing those individuals who can undertake this transformation is the central purpose of talent identification and development.

As well as leading the core purpose of student performance improvement, we need leaders who have the abilities and potential to deal with a variety of challenges that are on the current and future education landscape, such as: working across organisational boundaries with other agencies; extended schools; the Every Child Matters agenda; the 14–19 learning agenda; sustainable schools and new patterns of leadership and governance. How can we identify those individuals who have the capacity to take on these challenges? We will look next at distinguishing between current performance in a particular role and future leadership potential.

Are individuals ready for leadership?

It is obviously worthwhile to enable aspirant leaders to reflect on their readiness for leadership as well as to have other colleagues' views on them. The following is a useful self-inventory that we have used on leadership consultancy activities:

Readiness for a leadership role

Indicate your response using the three-point scale: 1 = disagree; 2 = neutral; 3 = agree.

1.	I enjoy having people rely on me for ideas and suggestions.	1	2	3
2.	I believe I inspire other people.	1	2	3
3.	It's important for me to compliment others on their efforts.	1	2	3
4.	Team success is more important than my personal recognition.	1	2	3
5.	Resolving conflict is an activity I actively engage in.	1	2	3
6.	I would enjoy coaching other members of the team.	1	2	3
7.	Building team spirit is critically important.	1	2	3
8.	The problems of the colleagues in my team are my problems too.	1	2	3
9.	Seeing the 'big picture' is vitally important.	1	2	3
10.	Team members value my contributions.	1	2	3

Total score: _____

Reflect on your score:

25–30	high readiness for leadership
20–25	moderate readiness for leadership
10–20	some doubts about readiness for leadership
10 or less	low readiness for leadership

Performance is not the same as potential

How do we ensure that people are given the right job for their present abilities and opportunities to develop their future potential? The more schools we visit, the more we recognise that leadership really matters – how people are treated, the values that are seen in action and other aspects of our leadership model determine whether staff are happy and motivated or unhappy and not motivated. The context is most important in determining what happens to potential talent, or even in recognising that there is talent. This is because potential is context-specific. It is the difference between an individual's current abilities and the future leadership needs of their school and how that difference will be overcome. In our experience, crucial to this are:

Values:	clear and inclusive, recognising everyone's contribution
Working with people:	staff knowing what is expected of them and that their views are listened to
Personal qualities:	staff receiving recognition for good work
Strategic acumen:	staff having opportunities to learn.

If people understand the key behaviours for a future role and have the opportunity to practise them, they would be more aware of whether a leadership post would be for them. For example, if the key behaviours for a particular leadership role are determined to be:

➤ take the lead in initiating ideas
➤ ensure people are committed to whole-school objectives
➤ challenge people to achieve more
➤ make careful risk assessments

then staff members would know if that job motivates and challenges them and if they have the potential to undertake the new responsibilities. In Chapter 3, we established that it is possible to be the best performer in one role but not have the self-motivation or skills for a new role or not have the opportunities to develop the skills for that new role. Performance is not the same as potential.

It is also worth pausing to consider the nature of the leadership roles that those with potential aspire to be able to achieve. Emerging leaders developing in the 21st century are unlikely to aspire to traditional roles of leadership. The all-consuming 'heroic leader' models may appear ineffective and more sustainable leadership roles need to be the ones that are articulated and defined if we are to have suitable applicants.

What does potential look like?

The first task in the successful management of potential is to define what we mean by potential. How might we recognise it? We have already established that potential will be affected by the person's attitude and the opportunities they receive. However, it is still possible to detect early signs of potential leaders through the person having credible mastery of their present role, having confidence, having the ability to see the 'big picture', being able to make connections and having the ability to get involved. It is important to identify characteristics of potential leaders rather than rely on someone's gut reaction or the person's own expression of the desire to be a leader.

The NCSL (2009), in a perceptive account of what 'talent managers' across different organisational sectors looked for in identifying those individuals who had the ability to develop leadership characteristics termed 'growth factors', articulated the following insights:

1. They can be recognised early – leadership factors could be discerned in a variety of situations such as the ability to think beyond immediate boundaries.
2. These growth factors are useful in a variety of leadership settings, such as demonstrating an eagerness to learn and try new ways of working.
3. They can be used to accelerate development – focus on individuals who already show characteristics that are difficult to develop, such as emotional resilience, because knowledge and skills are much easier for these individuals to develop.
4. Leadership characteristics that have limited downside, for example self-confidence, are considered to be good but overriding personal ambition and arrogance can be counterproductive.

Talent identification

We need to consider the processes and activities which will define and discover the sources of talent. Attracting people to the organisation is not the same as attracting the right people, those who will be enthusiastic, highly capable and loyal to the values, beliefs and mission of the organisation. Most significantly, we should ask how we identify 'hidden talent' in the organisation which to date has gone unrecognised. Organisations need to focus on the requirements for individuals to be successful in specific roles in their current and future contexts. Organisations are 'operating in increasingly dynamic environments', and to be 'truly successful they need to stay one step ahead of the game and predict who will be the key drivers of their future success' (Hay Group, 2005: 9). So the best organisations are future focused and predict what skills, attitudes and behaviours they will need from their talented individuals. If we need to be clear about what it means to be effective in the role and what talent looks like, we need to consider this in the specific context of our own school or organisation. The reader can now reflect on leadership roles in their own school:

> ### Reflection point on 'identification'
>
> This leadership role needs...
> Our best people are...

We need to be clear about which people have the potential to be leaders; this depends on the needs of the organisation and the nature of the work. Many definitions of the characteristics of 'talent' are available (CIPD, 2006; Cross, 2007; Hay Group, 2008; Peters, 2005; Thorne and Pellent, 2007) which we have organised into our framework:

How a person thinks

A talented performer:

➤ has the ability to understand the 'big picture' and make links
➤ has the ability to take on new roles successfully
➤ has the ability to take initiative and be a self-starter
➤ has the intellectual curiosity and flexibility to think differently
➤ has the ability to problem solve.

Peters (2005) considers that we need to pursue 'mastery' where we previously aimed to develop competence. The idea of mastery is interesting, described by Gilbert (2002) as a form of internal motivation, in Japanese culture, as the process of trying to be better 'than no one other than yourself'.

How a person works with others

A talented performer 'creates with' rather than 'delivers to' and:

➤ is self-confident and credible in role
➤ inspires others, shows caring and concern for others
➤ demonstrates empathy and has the ability to learn from others
➤ has a passion to make a difference.

A good frame of reference for this is John Novak's (2009) approach to 'invitational leadership' where inviting others personally and professionally promotes a 'doing with' rather than a 'doing to' which often means 'doing in'.

How flexible a person is

A talented performer:

➤ is resilient and knows how to finish the job
➤ craves action and gets involved
➤ endures confusion and has a willingness to embrace ambiguity
➤ takes advantage of opportunities.

These three elements provide a valuable framework for the evaluation of potential. Hay Group (2008: 7) believes that 'being a top performer in one's current job, or expressing great personal ambition and drive are not particularly good predictors of long term potential'. They assert that ambitious, achievement-orientated, self-confident people often have a short-term focus, arrogance, an inability to listen and a lack of self-control. This does not fit with the elements of being an effective leader which focuses on open and honest communication, humility, the creation of trust, self-awareness and flexibility. Performance in one role is not necessarily a good predictor of ability in another, i.e. excellent teachers don't always make good heads. It is important to separate the idea of performance from the notion of potential. The reader can now reflect on whether there is, for them, a correlation in their school between performance in one role and performance in another.

Outstanding research – Hay Group's (2008) *Rush to the Top*

In an outstanding piece of research on the topic of talent management, the Hay Group's *Rush to the Top* presents a compelling analysis. Hay Group (2008: 7) suggests that among head teachers, the traits they commonly identified as 'early warning signs for leadership potential' include:

➤ confidence and credibility
➤ the ability to see the 'big picture', to make connections and think of the whole school
➤ mastering the basics of their role quickly and looking for more
➤ getting involved (doesn't look the other way or walk past incidents)
➤ initiative and self-motivation (the sort of people you can't stop from leading)
➤ intellectual curiosity and capacity (sees the common threads)
➤ resilience and empathy (to survive the pace of acceleration and learn from others).

The Hay Group (2008: 11) also identified the characteristics of those who did not demonstrate leadership potential:

➤ a short-term focus on immediate results or acquiring technical expertise, at the expense of building capacity or acquiring breadth of experience
➤ arrogance or an assumption of being smarter than one's peers
➤ the inability to listen to others
➤ a lack of self-control and self-awareness.

Using the framework that we put forward, which sees potential as: how a person thinks, how a person works with others and how flexible a person is, combined with the insights from the Hay Group research, readers could undertake the following reflection:

Reflection point on identifying talent

What characteristics would you include in the identification of leadership 'potential' for a particular leadership role in your school?

How do the characteristics differ for middle and senior leadership roles?

Identifying and matching performance and potential – the nine-box grid

Potential is not an absolute measurement but the nine-box grid is a useful tool for the identification of leadership potential. The horizontal axis focuses on the performance management process and requires a judgement of the person's performance. The vertical axis requires a subjective qualitative assessment of leadership behaviours or potential.

The effectiveness of the tool is determined by the level of honest debate from the leadership team, to place each member of staff in one of the nine boxes. Each box comes with a level of support and required development, but the people in the top right hand box will be the focus for leadership talent development.

Four types of employee – A, B, C and D – can be identified and mapped on to the nine-box grid.

A. These are the outstanding leaders in your school. They are the individuals who consistently deliver exceptional practice and who inspire and influence the motivation of others. They demonstrate their ability to move on to higher leadership positions by the way they lead and interact with others. They are worth considerable investment of time and resources to deliver their potential for your organisation.

B. These are individuals who either:
   (Bi) have exceptional leadership potential but need to demonstrate exceptional performance credibility with their colleagues in order to be seen as successful school leaders. <u>Or</u>
   (Bii) individuals who exceed performance expectations but may not have had significant leadership opportunities to develop their leadership potential. Alternatively, they may see themselves as the pedagogic expert and have limited leadership ambition.

For both Bi and Bii individuals, the development time will be longer than with the A individuals and although the investment of time and resources will be justified, it will need to be evaluated as progress is made in order that a suitable return is evident.

C. These are solid performers who are the backbone of the organisation, who will get on with the job but will not drive change in the school. They will need professional updating but resource allocation for extensive leadership development would not be justified.

D. These are the under-performers in the organisation. They need performance management on improving either basic skills or their attitude or commitment to the organisation. The former will often be part of competency proceedings. With the latter, we picked up a phrase when working with principals in Los Angeles who describe those who are not committed and sometimes undermine the school leadership as 'mission incompatibles'! Their performance needs to radically improve and resources should be spent on this but if it fails to achieve the desired effect, individuals should be managed out of the organisation with no further resources committed.

Leadership Potential	Performance: Not met	Performance: Met	Performance: Exceeded
Exceeded		**Bi** — Capable of growth	**A** — Future leader / Outstanding
Met		**C** — Solid performer	**Bii** — Transferrable pedagogic skills but need leadership development
Not met	**D** — High risk / Performance manage or out		**C** — Expert talent / Trusted professional
	Not met	Met	Exceeded
	Performance Expectations		

Figure 4.1 *Leadership potential and performance expectations*

Michaels et al. (2001) identify the need to differentiate between people and summarise our view that leaders need to take different actions by:

A. investing in the A players
B. affirming and developing the B players
C. improving/raising the game of the C players or removing them from critical positions
D. removing the D players from the organisation.

Reflection point on matching performance and potential

Use the nine-box grid to define the A, B, C and D people in your school.

Leadership lessons from schools

We have provided an outline of some of the key concepts to engender a discussion about identifying leadership talent in your school or schools in general. We add richness to this discussion by drawing on leadership voices from the participants in our research project. These insights from practice by leaders of special, secondary and primary schools follow next.

Insight from practice: a special school principal

One special school looks for characteristics which may indicate talent through the evaluation of actions and attributes demonstrated in a whole-school initiative.

We are constantly on the lookout for staff who have a greater than expected impact on a whole-school initiative, who have responded to a challenge, managed time well and hit the deadlines. These staff members have gone the extra mile in their commitment and can see their impact for themselves and enjoy the buzz of their success. We also look to see who has exhibited some of the following characteristics:

➤ is focused and determined
➤ is surefooted – having the knowledge and knowing where they are going and how to get there
➤ shows initiative and has analytical and problem-solving skills
➤ has innovative ideas
➤ is credible and inspirational – can model and get other staff on board
➤ has stamina and resilience to follow up, follow through and see something completed, with a mental toughness not to be deterred
➤ can take short-term actions compatible with a long-term goal
➤ is at ease explaining and articulating process and outcome.

In analysing and evaluating a whole-school initiative, we identify who was able to link things and see the bigger picture. We ask the question 'Who was critical to its success?'

Insight from practice: a secondary school principal

This secondary school sees that 'talent' is in the spotting of it. They concentrate on the ability of potential leaders to influence the practice of others.

The leaders of school organisations have to have their radar adjusted to recognise those colleagues with the flair to make a real difference, not only in their own classrooms and teams but also in the classrooms and teams of others. This is one of the starting points for talent spotting: the degree to which one individual can influence the practice of another in a positive and practical manner.

As a leader of a federation, there are three key indicators that keep me alert to the talent of people I work with, in addition to the starting point outlined above.

➤ The degree to which a colleague can operate effectively within the confines of the school building, and outside it. This could be in the virtual world, as well as in the district, regional or national arenas.
➤ The degree to which a colleague becomes a significant presence in the school, so that their absence is noticed when they are not around for whatever reason. They are reliable and support the wider activities of the school and go beyond their core role as, for example, a teacher of biology.
➤ The degree of confidence they have in themselves and that which they inspire in others whether this is parents, children, visitors, peers or school leaders.

Good talent management helps people to believe in themselves. Changing behaviour, as we know when trying to influence children to change their behaviour, takes time. It is also critical that the person understands their present behaviour and understands the need to change. With children, using the language of choice is vital in order for children to understand what they are doing, how their behaviour is perceived by others and what the consequences of their choices are for themselves and for others. So too with talent, performance improvement is enabled by the member of staff understanding what they are doing, how that is perceived and what the impact is of their choices. This is why coaching is a key element of performance improvement, a concept which will be further developed in Chapter 6.

Insight from practice: a primary school principal

How do we help people become the best they can be? The following primary school example describes the opportunities given to two potential leaders and what affected the consequences.

Lucy and Susan both had potential, as determined through the performance-management process and their mastery in their present roles. Through an optional performance review, both Lucy and Susan had

(Continues)

(Continued)

shown a willingness to undertake new challenges and both expressed a desire to move to leadership roles. Lucy was not convinced that she could do it, while Susan felt it was her right.

The following had been identified as important to new leadership roles in school and were identified as behaviours to be developed by both Susan and Lucy. Neither had previously had the opportunity to demonstrate their skill in these areas:

➢ Observation and evaluation of colleagues' practice.
➢ Constructive feedback to team members on their performance.
➢ Leading an initiative for change.
➢ Explanation of an initiative for governors.

Lucy was motivated to start the process and requested to be coached through a series of observations and feedback sessions with both teacher and support staff in the team in which she worked. She researched examples of effective feedback and the language to use for constructive feedback. She initiated discussion of this and wanted to discuss the effect of her practice, seeking feedback herself and responding positively to points for development. The team members who were observed found her credible, trustworthy and truthful. She developed the ability to give hard feedback and always supported the member of staff as they worked to improve practice. Lucy showed huge potential and increased in self-confidence. Leading others gave her great satisfaction and motivation. Susan too participated in the coaching programme for observation and feedback, but whilst she was skilled at giving positive feedback she was reluctant to discuss points for development with her team colleagues. Her desire to be liked overrode the behaviours needed for good leadership. Susan was reluctant to give extra time and did not demonstrate any intellectual curiosity.

Both change initiatives were successful at team level but Susan was unable to see the impact of the change beyond her team and reluctant to admit any fault on behalf of her team, while being only too willing to celebrate the fault of other teams in school as the reason for lack of impact beyond her team. Lucy's change was successful at team level and she had investigated how her team could support the wider take-up of the initiative, describing how she would support the change in other teams. Lucy was able to understand and describe the bigger picture to governors. She actively listened to their views and was willing to admit when she didn't know the answer. She knew what she wanted to do next to challenge team members to achieve more.

Lucy went on to be an outstanding deputy head. Susan remains as part of a team which is difficult to integrate into the whole school.

What do these insights from practice tell us? In all cases, the leaders have moved on from simple succession planning to the identification of talented individuals as a key for organisational success. They have identified key criteria about what makes talented individuals and how they can be identified. The final case study illustrates the delight of developing an A performer and also the frustration of not always being able to succeed in the move of a B performer from a pedagogic to a whole-school role.

The critical importance of talent development

The Hay Group (2008) suggested that the top chief executives in the corporate world spend 50 per cent of their time mentoring, coaching and developing the next generation of leaders. It is unlikely that head teachers in busy schools would claim to spend the same amount of time on this but it is worth reflecting on how important the identification and development of leadership talent is and how much time they do spend on it.

Reflection point on talent identification and development

> How significant in terms of time and other resources is the talent identification process in your school?
> How much time do you personally spend on talent development?

Within the education system, an often quoted statistic is that 50 per cent of teachers who qualify and start teaching leave after five years of teaching. Clearly, many do a good job and move on to different careers and roles in their life, some obviously to return at a later date. However, some will have left because they worked in schools with poor leadership and inadequate mentoring and support systems. What would the parallel be in the leadership potential domain? The most confident and articulate staff often force themselves to 'centre stage' to seek recognition and gain promotion and development. Very often this is rightly so. But what do leaders do to ensure the leaders with personal and professional modesty are recognised and developed in assisting a powerful learning pool of talent for the school? The difference between level-4 and level-5 leaders in Jim Collins' (2001) terms is a salutary lesson here. The level-4 leaders have high levels of drive but are often self-publicists who, while effective in the short term, do not leave sustainable leadership practices in school. The level-5 leaders, on the other hand, have personal modesty but also determined and strong levels of professional will to challenge current orthodoxies to do the best for the school. As a result, they leave sustainable leadership and schools. We need to identify those leaders who have the potential to be level-5 leaders.

Conclusion

We hope that this chapter has provided the reader with insights and perspectives to enable them to reflect on the most challenging issue in talent management of determining current performance and future potential. The well-known 'Peters principle' where individuals are promoted to their level of incompetence is a stark reminder of avoiding the tendency to promote individuals the longer they are in the organisation and seniority determining advancement. Being able to articulate key leadership attributes and skills for particular posts and identifying whether those staff who express the desire for advancement actually have the attributes and skills is an immensely difficult challenge for leaders of school.

Suggested further reading

Hay Group (2008) *Rush to the Top*. London: Hay Group.

Leithwood, K., Day, C., Sammons, P., Harris, A. and Hopkins, D. (2006) *Seven Strong Claims about Successful School Leadership*. Nottingham: NCSL.

NCSL (2009) *What are we Learning about Identifying Talent – Evidence into Practice Guide*. Nottingham: NCSL.

To assess where the reader is in terms of their own organisation, the following self-reflection exercise is based on the four elements of our leadership model: values, personal qualities, working with others and strategic acumen. The reader may wish to review it with a colleague.

Talent assessment framework: performance or potential?

Rate yourself (in partnership discussion) on the following categories.

1 = not at all; 2 = only partially; 3 = to a degree; 4 = very often; 5 = completely

Values

Are your staff equally valued whether or not they have leadership potential?	1 2 3 4 5
If potential leaders receive more resources for professional learning, do you promote staff understanding for this?	1 2 3 4 5

Personal qualities

Is your school able to objectively identify ABCD people?	1 2 3 4 5
Are staff in your school motivated to take on leadership roles?	1 2 3 4 5

Working with others

Does the leadership team work together to identify people with potential?	1 2 3 4 5
Do all staff understand the characteristics which define effective leadership in your school?	1 2 3 4 5

Strategic acumen

Does your school have a clear way of identifying potential?	1 2 3 4 5
Is talent identification a key element of your school strategy?	1 2 3 4 5

Those items you have rated 1 or 2 would need to be developed while those ranked 4 or 5 need to be celebrated and sustained. Those rated 3 warrant further reflection.

Section 2

Talent Development

Chapter 5

Talent development

This chapter considers:

- developing leadership
- evaluating your leadership skills – portfolio exercises
- learning activities to develop talent
- a five-stage process to deepen understanding of leadership development
- stages in leadership development.

There are severable debatable issues when considering talent development. First, we need to consider whether talent development is a process which should be restricted to a small percentage of staff who have been identified as 'talented' or whether it is a process which should apply to all staff. Second, we should consider whether it is an open and transparent process where staff know what 'talent assessment' has been made about them so they can be involved in their own assessments and development strategies, or whether it is a process which is undertaken by senior management in a confidential way with only the outcomes published. Third, we should consider if it is possible to enable talent development for a focused few and still provide equality of opportunity for all. Schools need to reflect on these issues when they establish their own process for talent development.

It is important to consider:

Reflection point

- What is in place for the development of all staff?
- Where does talent enablement fit in?

The development of leadership learning and of leadership skills are the most important capabilities for a talent-focused organisation. A dynamic and effective organisation will have a well-established process for the professional learning of all staff, which is effectively connected with other key processes such as performance management. All processes should work together and be integrated, for example effective performance management and professional reviews should be a starting point for staff learning and development.

Talent development requires a clearly defined structure of leadership roles which grow in responsibility and impact. A talent development process needs a clear understanding about the characteristics and behaviours associated with success at each level of leadership. Ideally, a school should ensure that there is a steady flow of people through these leadership roles in order that there are staff who are ready to move to a different position when the occasion arises. This may involve letting a talented leader leave if there are no appropriate opportunities in the school through which to challenge and develop them.

If we accept that potential leaders need to be self-motivated and thrive on challenges, we believe it is vital that there is open and honest communication with people about the assessments of their potential. So in the debate of whether the process should be honest and open, we believe that talent development cannot happen in secret. Leaders need to regularly evaluate the progress of colleagues and be ready to provide support and development opportunities when a potential leader encounters gaps in their knowledge, skills, attitudes or behaviour. The potential leader should be active in this process.

The development of talented individuals is often associated with accelerated development. We believe that any acceleration of development must also take account of the participant's personal development as well as their professional learning. Research from the Hay Group (2008) suggested that current leaders are stronger than emerging leaders in respect of:

> ➤ their vision
> ➤ their political awareness
> ➤ their ability to influence indirectly
> ➤ their ability to build alliances
> ➤ their long-term thinking and planning.

NCSL (2008) claim that abilities, as outlined by the Hay Group, are often associated with experience and maturity, which sets a challenge for accelerated talent development programmes since leadership maturity needs to be accelerated as well as professional skills. The areas, identified by the Hay Group, cover all aspects of our leadership development model, those of personal qualities, of strategic acumen and of working with others. It is rare therefore for an inexperienced, immature professional to be able to act in a leadership role whatever their potential. It is important to provide opportunities for potential leaders to develop personally and professionally before they undertake a leadership role. We have all seen the 'whizz kid' newly appointed head fail because he doesn't have the necessary personal behaviours to be effective in the role.

Personal qualities are most important and may be a key to identifying young, inexperienced potential leaders. We have established, in Chapter 4, that skill and knowledge can be learned but we believe that personal behaviours are more difficult to develop. The following assessment exercises will provide a vehicle for the self-evaluation of personal behaviours or could be used as a focus for the potential leader in discussion with a leadership coach. Firstly, we look at the important dimension of behaving ethically. Leaders influence others by what they say and what they do. The dimension of moral leadership is one that underpins the whole value system of the school. The following inventory, although amusing at times, provides an interesting discussion point if all members of the leadership team undertake it and compare their results. In our consultancy work, we have had participants with scores in each of the categories. It is easy to answer the questions with the 'right' answer but there is no learning in that, so try to answer the questions honestly for your own behaviour.

Assessment exercise 1: ethical behaviour

Describe how well you agree with each of the statements. Use the following scale:
5 = strongly disagree, 4 = disagree, 3 = neutral, 2 = agree, 1 = strongly agree

1. When applying for a new role, I would cover up the fact that I had been unsuccessful in a similar role.   5 4 3 2 1

2. Making a few pounds through expenses is ok.   5 4 3 2 1

3. It is acceptable to read the e-mail messages and notes for other staff.   5 4 3 2 1

4. Employees should not inform on each other for wrongdoing.   5 4 3 2 1

(Continues)

5. It is acceptable to give approximate figures on expense sheets if you don't have to submit receipts.   5 4 3 2 1

6. I see no problem with conducting a little personal business on school time.   5 4 3 2 1

7. If I received £500 for doing extra tuition I would not report it on my income tax return.   5 4 3 2 1

8. I see no harm in taking home a few school supplies for my personal use.   5 4 3 2 1

9. If I am very pressed for time, it would be acceptable to have a colleague write a report for me.   5 4 3 2 1

10. It is acceptable to call in sick in order to take a day off, if I only do it once or twice a year.   5 4 3 2 1

11. I would accept a permanent, full-time job even if I knew that I only wanted the job for six months.   5 4 3 2 1

12. I would not check school policy before accepting an expensive gift from a parent or supplier.   5 4 3 2 1

13. At work, if it gets me out of trouble, I don't tell the truth all the time.   5 4 3 2 1

14. I would authorise accepting a school resource on a 30-day trial period, even if I knew we had no intention of buying it.   5 4 3 2 1

15. Just to make a promotion, I would stretch the truth about a previous successful achievement.   5 4 3 2 1

Now add up the numbers you have circled to get a total score:

65–75 – You are a strongly ethical person.

30–64 – You show average awareness of ethical issues – are there any key areas to be improved?

21–29 – Your ethics are underdeveloped – in order to be more effective, you need to be more sensitive to ethical issues.

15–20 – Are you in the right job?

A person's emotional and social effectiveness are vital for any leadership role. Good leaders have a significant degree of self-awareness – they know and understand their emotions and the effect these emotions have on other people. It is also a key to effective self-awareness to be confident and dynamic while not being over zealous. This leads on to the fact that effective leaders can engage in realistic self-management which involves managing their own emotions and so not getting too depressed when things do not work out, while retaining the ability to stay positive and balanced in challenging circumstances. The impact a leader has on others and how they treat other people is the key to the wider social awareness that leaders need so they can be sensitive and responsive to others and understand individual and group needs. The second assessment point considers aspects of these skills.

Assessment exercise 2: personal understanding

Emotional awareness
1. How emotionally self-aware are you?
2. Are you able to make accurate self-evaluations?
3. Are you self-confident in your role?

Self-management
4. Do you demonstrate self-control in difficult situations?
5. When are you conscientious? Are there any activities when you are not?
6. Do you find it easy to be adaptable?
7. When have you taken the initiative for something?

Social skills
8. How have you demonstrated empathy towards someone in your team?
9. How have you supported the development of others in your team?
10. How have you managed a conflict situation?
11. How have you developed your networking skills?

The third assessment exercise looks at a person's ability to reflect and how much attention is given to their own personal growth. This assessment point is designed to encourage you to reflect on behaviours characteristic of a personally effective leader. How leaders develop themselves as leaders and learners has a key impact on their approach to influencing others both directly and indirectly.

Assessment exercise 3: personal effectiveness

For each statement, indicate how accurately it describes you – be honest and base your answers on your actual behaviour. Use the following scale:
1=rarely, 2=occasionally, 3=most often

1. I believe that it is a core part of my role to build and develop effective relationships with colleagues.	1	2	3
2. I am able to describe what my key interpersonal strengths are.	1	2	3
3. I seek to learn and develop new skills every year.	1	2	3
4. I discuss my personal development with friends, colleagues or mentors.	1	2	3
5. I have a clear understanding of how my behaviour and attitude impact on others in a range of different contexts.	1	2	3
6. I am able to clearly articulate the values that are the basis for my professional judgements and behaviours.	1	2	3
7. I can evidence examples of where my moral purpose is embedded in my day-to-day practice.	1	2	3
8. I encourage an environment where colleagues feel comfortable being challenged and in challenging what we do.	1	2	3
9. I have a strong curiosity about how other leaders, within and outside my team, lead their teams and organisations.	1	2	3
10. I make sure that I have opportunities outside my professional life to nurture other curiosities, passions and personal relationships.	1	2	3
11. I regularly make time to reflect upon my personal skills and my leadership styles.	1	2	3
12. I regularly read articles, papers, books or blogs that will contribute to my personal development.	1	2	3
13. I articulate my reflections upon my professional life and personal practice through a professional journal.	1	2	3
14. I question my own assumptions and encourage others to question theirs.	1	2	3
15. I am not afraid to challenge 'the way we do things' in my organisation.	1	2	3

Now add up the numbers you have circled to get a total score:

36–45 You are personally effective.

26–35 You show average effectiveness – are there any key areas to be improved?

15–25 Your personal effectiveness could be developed. Consider:

> ➤ What have you learned about areas to be further developed?

> ➤ How will you do it?

> ➤ Who will you get to support you?

Learning activities to develop talent

Leaders have increased responsibility for managing others and potential leaders will need to develop skills associated with enabling others to succeed and learn. Some learning activities offer more opportunity for potential leaders to develop personal skills and behaviours and include:

Job shadowing and working with the school leadership team

Job shadowing is an activity which enables a potential leader to learn about a leadership role by being a shadow to an effective leader through the working day or through a particular experience. Potential leaders witness at first hand the work environment and professional occupational skills in action. Job shadowing is designed to increase awareness, to help model behaviour through examples and reinforce the link between theoretical learning and practice. This is why it is best for someone to job shadow an effective role model. Job shadowing is based on observation and will only be effective if the potential leader has the skills of observation and evaluation. Job shadowing has the potential to develop new skills and develop a better understanding of the role and organisation. Job shadowing could also help an organisation when considering succession planning and retention, but it is important to be clear about the function before setting it up. For a potential leader, the effectiveness of the leader they observe in a coaching role is key to the amount of learning they will gain from the experience.

Mentoring or coaching to support the interpretation of experiences

Many schools use mentoring to support the induction of newly appointed staff. Mentoring can also support progression, support a person in a new role or in undertaking a new challenge and provide the personal support needed in a new learning situation. Mentors are experienced colleagues who can access a range of self-directed opportunities. Mentors provide personal support, reflection and facilitation.

In contrast, a coach provides knowledge and experience. Potential leaders gain value from receiving coaching as well as learning how to act as a coach. It is important that a coach is respected and has credibility with the coached colleague because a coach should be able to promote and enhance reflective practice. Coaches need to be able to:

> develop mutual understanding
> observe and discuss practice
> interpret evidence
> make sense of issues
> make decisions about the best way forward
> actively listen
> deal with conflict.

All these skills and abilities are necessary for potential leaders. Sense making is a core professional ability and involves the ability to apply expertise and clarify values and vision to finding solutions in problematic issues. Expert leaders are better able to articulate and prioritise issues and have a clear and considered awareness. They are more able to integrate strategic and operational thinking. Leadership coaching helps potential leaders clarify their visions, beliefs and values, and stretches their capacity to lead and influence.

Co-coaching could be a useful process for developing leaders, where both participants are professional learners who have a commitment to reciprocal learning and give non-judgemental support of each other based on the evidence from their own practice.

Job change in order to work in unfamiliar contexts or roles

A job change can offer potential leaders important learning experiences; this may be to work in a partner school or to work in their own school in a different context. The opportunity will give the potential leader experience of using their skills within different teams or in a changed context. The role may be short term, where observation and discussion will be important, or could be longer term with some project to be achieved, such as supporting the introduction of an initiative in a different setting. The learning from these experiences would be enhanced through the potential leader having the support of a coach to facilitate their reflection and evaluation. This approach is made easier if the school is part of a wider partnership of schools. This will be discussed more fully in Chapter 9 where we consider talent development by an individual school or through a wider system.

Participation in school-wide initiatives

Some potential leaders are not in a position to influence others. One way of giving them the experience of leading other people is to give them the opportunity to lead a school-wide initiative for a specified length of time. For example, a potential leader may be asked to lead the introduction of a one-to-one learning support school-wide initiative for student achievement or may be given the opportunity to lead a longer-term project to target underachieving students. The responsibility must be genuine, with the potential leader having the opportunity to manage the resources allocated for the project and given the opportunity to make decisions. Skills of using evidence and finding solutions will be needed and additional support may be necessary to enable this learning. The responsibilities and expected outcomes must be clearly established before the learning experience begins.

A deeper understanding of leadership development

In the context of professional development, there is a distinction between horizontal and vertical development. Both are important, but they occur at different rates. Horizontal growth happens through training or self-directed learning or simply through life experiences. Vertical development in adults is much rarer. It refers to how we change our interpretations of experience and how we transform our views of reality. It corresponds to an increase in awareness, of what we pay attention to and therefore what we influence. In general, transformations of human perception or changes in world view are more powerful than any amount of horizontal growth and learning. The development of potential towards deeper understanding, wisdom and effectiveness occurs in a logical sequence of stages. This movement is often likened to a spiral. A person's stage of development influences what they notice or can become aware of and, therefore, what they can articulate, influence and change. As a leader develops, there is an increased tolerance for difference and ambiguity as well as increased flexibility, reflection and skill in interacting with the environment. Leadership development stages are useful because they provide a way of understanding how leaders tend to interpret events and, thus, how they are likely to act in a given situation or conflict. Although people may have access to several stages as part of their repertoire, they tend to respond spontaneously with the most complex one they have available. Under pressure and rapid change conditions, people often resort to behaviour patterns from earlier stages. A development perspective aids our understanding of learning which may lead to more effectiveness.

Daniel Goleman (2000) uses different levels of emotional intelligence to describe various leadership styles and offers an interesting mix between leadership style and developmental stage. His research showed that leaders with the greatest emotional intelligence, those with most self-awareness, self-management and social skills had the most positive effect on working culture and climate. We discuss the importance of the culture of the school in Chapter 8.

Benzia et al. (2001) describe a model for stages of leadership based on the development of an effective environment. It shows that the foundation for creating this type of organisation begins with building an environment of trust. These researchers assert that stages cannot be missed out, for example that you cannot have meaningful transformations without alignment, or you cannot have empowerment without trust. The following model, based on Benzia et al. (2001), identifies the leadership development needed to build transformation.

We have already discussed that when there is trust and mutual respect, people feel supported by the leadership and safe to be empowered. When people are empowered, they feel free to express their individual talent. When there is open communication and collaboration, people can translate their individual talent into more powerful collective results. When there is alignment and commitment around a compelling organisational purpose, the collaborative energy and talent of individual people can be channelled to achieve transformational outcomes. It is possible to identify the leadership skills needed to develop each stage of the model.

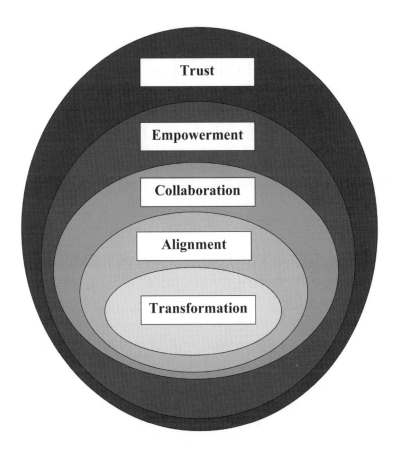

Figure 5.1 *Leadership development needed to build transformation (based on Benzia et al., 2001)*

Stage 1: Leadership skills which are needed to build a climate of trust

Walk the talk. As a leader, you must be authentic to inspire the trust of your colleagues. It is not enough to set the values and standards for your organisation – you must live those values and standards in every aspect of your behaviour. It is also important to know how your colleagues perceive your behaviour.

Trust yourself first. Leaders should show confidence in their own leadership abilities and competencies. The ability to take tough stands to support your principles is a key skill. At the root of many communication difficulties or social problems is a lack of trust which often starts with a leader's lack of trust in themselves, for example when leaders are afraid of their own anger. Trust grows as we keep our promises.

Have a genuine interest in others. Rapport and shared values help create a context for building trust more quickly.

Be willing to hear and say the good and the bad. Trust can be deepened and often re-established when people talk about difficult issues, especially when people do so with a constructive attitude. When we fail to trust others, we tend to treat them in subtle ways that are not only unconstructive, but which destroy relationships. This works both ways.

Stage 2: Leadership skills which help to build an environment which empowers people

Create an environment of experiential learning. Learning happens when behaviour changes. To create a learning organisation, a leader must have systems and underlying principles that continually empower the entire team.

Encourage continual learning. Great ideas are simply not enough. Empowerment is credible when people have the training and experience in order to make significant contributions. This must be an ongoing process.

Coach your colleagues. When people are properly coached, they feel empowered and capable. When you tell people what to do, however well intended, you diminish their sense of power and responsibility. Instead of telling, ask powerful questions that bring out the best ideas and solutions that people have.

Create an environment where everyone wants to contribute. Recognise the opinions and contributions of others. Leaders need to be willing to suspend their beliefs and to listen deeply for the meaning in conversations with people. They need to come from a perspective of not knowing the solution and be able to listen for the emotions behind the words, acknowledging their own feelings and those of others.

Be a democratic leader. Give your colleagues real choices and the information to make informed choices. Leaders who see the value in democratic, self-organising systems can create a powerful context for learning and contributing.

Stage 3: Leadership skills which establish organisational values that encourage collaboration

Declare the intent to create a culture that values and supports collaboration and regularly engage in dialogue with your leadership team and staff team. Provide the time for formal and informal communications. Provide processes and management systems that encourage, support and reward collaborative efforts.

Have a compelling and audacious goal that motivates others. A purpose that motivates and stretches participants is the first necessary step for collaboration to take place.

Employ best-practice team dynamics. Fighting about issues is good; fighting other people is not only unproductive, but tends to be destructive and should be avoided. Frank and open dialogue should be encouraged.

Set high standards, and enforce them. Behavioural standards for team and project members should be decided as soon as the team begins to work together. Having the team develop a code of behaviour, for example for starting on time, keeping discussions confidential, one person talking at a time, etc. is important for ensuring high team performance. Teams that socialise get to know each other on a deeper level and consequently can work more effectively as a group.

Stage 4: Leadership skills which create organisational alignment

Express a compelling vision for a more desirable future. The right vision energises staff at all levels and provides a cause to align skills, talents and resources to make it happen. The vision should be communicated throughout the organisation.

Engage others in an ongoing visionary planning process. The more your colleagues participate in creating the vision and strategy, the more sense of ownership and alignment they will have for the organisational purpose. The result is much higher levels of performance from employees who are committed to excellence.

Have clear accountabilities for results. The best vision, mission and strategies will not be implemented without action. Ensure that responsibilities and accountabilities are well defined for each strategic objective and project. Clarify the roles that people have in the decision-making process, including approval, providing information, consulting or being informed.

Before you can change the organisation, you must change yourself. Culture is a very powerful force in any organisation, and as a leader you set the standard for organisational behaviour. To create an environment for organisational alignment, ensure that you and the leadership team are aligned with your organisation's vision and mission.

Stage 5: Leadership skills for transformational thinking

Build an environment that supports individual as well as team creativity. Transformational thinking is an ongoing process. Leaders need to be able to challenge and inspire staff.

Find a solution or part of a solution that can be tested and improved on a small scale. Then those who were involved in the success teach others, so the new methods can spread, allowing for improvements along the way. This approach tends to yield solutions that are very effective, and that continue to evolve and improve even while they are being implemented.

The following reflection point is an opportunity to consider the staged development of leadership skills as previously identified in Figure 5.1.

Reflection point: staged development of leadership skills

1. **Developing trust**
   Do others perceive every aspect of your behaviour, on or off the job, as completely trustworthy?
   Are you ready to confront others who are not trustworthy or ethical?
   How well do you know your colleagues?
   Are all colleagues able to constructively communicate something which is important? Do you and your leadership team say it all, constructively?
   What processes and management systems are in place to support leadership feedback?

2. **Empowerment**
   What systems do you have in place to empower colleagues?

Do you have concepts and ideas that sound great but which don't get fully tested or implemented?

Do you have the systems and training in place that empower all your colleagues to learn new and innovative approaches that will assist in the growth in your organisation or is there resistance even to positive change?

3. **Collaboration**

   Are your organisational goals really understood by all people at all levels?

   How are people selected to work on common goals?

   Can people self-select themselves to work on teams where they have passion and competence to significantly contribute?

4. **Alignment**

   Is your individual purpose in alignment with your organisational purpose?

   What about the rest of your colleagues?

   Do you know what your colleagues are passionate about?

   How can their passion and energy be harnessed to achieve organisational goals?

5. **Transformation**

   How does your school culture encourage experimentation and risk-taking by individuals as well as teams?

   How is open and authentic dialogue practised in your organisation?

   What opportunities for joint problem-solving do you provide?

Stages in leadership development

It is also possible to identify leadership steps which are the points of development through which a leader can perceive and act in reality. At each stage, the person's world view changes and expands. Each stage includes all of the abilities of the prior stages which begin to work together to develop a new level of complexity. Earlier stages may not have the combined cognitive, social, emotional or value-driven behaviours for the leader to perceive or act in an effective way.

1: Beginner leader

Someone beginning the journey of leadership operates functionally focusing on tasks and roles of leadership. The beginner leader demonstrates little situational perception or judgement and may react emotionally to situations, act alone and be unable to trust or develop trust. They tend not to question directives or frameworks.

2: Advanced beginner

Leadership performance should improve with experience and as more leadership situations are encountered. Understanding and situational perception improves but is still limited – all things are treated as if they are of equal importance. This leader acts and thinks in a linear way, and is operationally competent but their strategic awareness is limited.

3: Competent leader

This leader understands the scope and range of the role and is able to delegate and promote effective relationships. They are able to select and concentrate on the most important tasks and can discern longer-term goals. This leader is able to empower others and encourage collaboration.

4: Proficient leader

The proficient leader sees what is most important in situations and is able to build effective processes and relationships. They are able to involve others in the development of the strategic approach and encourage alignment of staff to the school's goals.

5: Expert leader

The expert leader has a repertoire of behaviours to deal with changing situations and often deals with complex problems in creative ways. They have a broader, more flexible and more imaginative perspective on the whole organisation and its context. They recognise multiple ways of framing reality and understand that personal and organisational change requires mutual, voluntary initiatives. They are able to identify and develop potential leaders. The expert leader has deeply held values which drive all actions and behaviours.

In addition to the variety of these learning practices, which are discussed in Chapter 6 and offer the opportunity for potential leaders to see what leadership is about, professional learning should be integrated with other human resource processes, should be purposeful and link with strategic intents and should have an impact.

However we define potential, talent is too often unfulfilled. Promising leaders, with many personal strengths and attributes, are too often diverted from achieving that potential. It is important that we understand what can cause the diversion. These factors can be school-based and are seen as:

➤ a lack of support during your change to a new leadership role
➤ a lack of early feedback on your impact in a new role
➤ not giving importance or prioritising self time to think and plan
➤ not having the confidence to act or not having the confidence not to act.

Personally based factors may also divert someone from taking up a leadership position and may include:

➤ changing personal situations and priorities
➤ the inability to listen to others
➤ a lack of self-control or awareness.

Making the change from being an individual contributor to the school to being a leader, whether of teaching staff or of support staff, most often happens in schools because of the person's individual mastery in their role. We have seen that these people are passionate about the job, are conscientious and want to acquire new skills. But these abilities do not help when leading other people. Leaders must learn to take pride in others' achievements and gain satisfaction from helping others to succeed. Leaders must be able to delegate and to trust colleagues to do the task. Because of the personal nature of these changes, support should be through induction, mentoring and coaching.

The NCSL research, *Review of the Landscape: Leadership and Leadership Development* (2008), provides evidence about effective leadership development. The research suggests that:

➤ approaches which focus on the work context and on the whole leadership team have greater impact on the school
➤ personalised programmes which focus on process rather than content are more likely to be transferred into practice.

The research focused on accelerated talent-development programmes and suggested that a key factor in determining satisfaction with programmes for those with high potential was 'clarity of expectation' both for the participants, their colleagues, coaches or schools hosting exchanges. The research suggested that:

➤ the commitment of the participant's school leadership team was a critical success factor where work-based learning was taking place

➤ where one-to-one coaching support was judged to be tailored to a participant's needs, satisfaction was highest.

These evaluations relate to participant satisfaction, but experience and what we know about motivation would tell us that they would also be key determinants to the effectiveness of such development programmes.

Our research has involved fascinating accounts of development in practice. We now draw on these by providing the following primary and secondary examples of leadership development.

Insight from practice – primary leadership

Jill was appointed as KS1 team leader after joining the school as Leader for a core curriculum area. Through performance review, which was an open and honest discussion with the head teacher, it was clear that Jill would like to work towards deputy headship. A range of school-based learning and opportunities were discussed to support this progression. Jill and the head were able to express their views about Jill's readiness to take on additional learning.

The head always articulated the leadership learning benefits to be gained from the school-based opportunity but Jill had time to think through the implications of any changes before agreeing the way forward. The school had in place a mentor programme for all staff, so Jill had been able to mentor teachers moving to different year groups and decided to take on the training for coaching and the opportunity to coach a newly appointed team leader, as this would give her the opportunity to develop new skills and behaviours. Jill took part in a school-based masters course which gave her the opportunity to undertake research projects linked with the school improvement plan. She was able to successfully introduce initiatives and lead the development of these changes through school. The head teacher coached her through meetings with difficult staff, giving her feedback on her handling of conflict situations. Jill was able to work shadow the school deputy head and took on some of his responsibilities in his absence. She was given time to think and reflect on the experiences and time to discuss with the head teacher. Jill was given the opportunity to observe governor meetings and subsequently was elected as staff governor. Jill also had the opportunity to lead sessions on using research in school for local teachers at the Educational Studies

---

Department of the local university. Jill kept a learning journal of critical incidents and her reflections on her learning.

Jill feels that her successful route to deputy headship was because of the learning opportunities offered to her in school but most importantly because of the coaching received, with the opportunity to reflect on experiences and discuss successes and areas for development.

In this case study, Jill used a reflective journal. It is useful to describe a critical incident and to identify the leadership skills and behaviours which led to a successful outcome. It is also useful to identify key competencies which could be further developed. Using the journal enables a potential leader to be reflective and increasingly more analytical about their own leadership skills, but this learning is enhanced if the work can be discussed with a coach who should bring further evaluation and a wider perspective to the area under discussion. As well as being an effective tool for personal development, the journal can document progress and achievement.

Insight from practice – secondary leadership

John had completed NPQH and had found the experience good in parts but thought that the approach was rather formulaic and that it lacked an in-depth approach to his own personal development. The school had a sophisticated approach to talent development and each potential leader was allocated a leadership coach. John was a senior head of faculty and was looking to move to a deputy headship post.

The leadership coach worked with John to establish a programme that would enhance his leadership experience and conceptual understanding of the deputy head role. John was given the opportunity to lead the introduction of a new curriculum for 16–19, reporting to the deputy for guidance and support. He was also asked to work alongside the deputy in charge of reviewing the 14–19 curriculum to make recommendations for the policy and strategy of the whole school.

The role of the coach was to meet John on a fortnightly basis to review the nature and dimensions of the leadership aspects of his two new responsibilities and to reflect on appropriate responses and strategies for the future. As part of an ongoing performance-management cycle, John was encouraged to review his leadership learning and to articulate his future development needs.

(Continues)

> *(Continued)*
>
> In terms of his team leadership and presentational skills, John was required to be an effective team leader and report both to staff meetings and governor meetings on curriculum development in this area. He was also closely involved with partnership working with other schools which allowed him to compare their practice with that of the school and to draw lessons from different leadership approaches and styles.
>
> John considers that the experience of leading a whole-school development, with the support of an effective coach to help him reflect, has given him a stronger experience base to apply for a future leadership position.

John found the school-based learning programme to be effective because it was tailored to his individual needs and gave contextual support through the process. He learnt a lot and was able to improve the leadership skills and leadership behaviours which had been identified for his leadership development.

The NCSL (2008) research suggested a checklist for the planning of talent development programmes which should ensure the programme:

➤ focuses on leadership behaviours which are likely to have most impact on pupil learning
➤ provides clear expectations for everyone involved in the programme
➤ is sensitive to the needs of potential leaders of different phases of education
➤ allows for personalisation.

Explicit performance-management processes are also seen as vital components both for those potential leaders on the programme and for their coaches and mentors. Performance management for the potential leader ensures that the individuals gain feedback on how they are progressing. Personalisation is realised through the use of effective coaches, and clear quality assurance should be in place to ensure that any coaching is successful. Any programme for potential leaders should ensure that opportunities are available, following the programme for the individual to continue along the leadership path. Talent development is a pre-condition for effective succession planning.

Conclusion

Our research, in schools and businesses, tells us that talent development requires:

> ➤ strategic acumen: integration into strategic plans
> ➤ working with others: active support and commitment of the school leadership team
> ➤ personal qualities needed for leadership
> ➤ core values which are actively lived.

Suggested further reading

Gay, M. and Sims, D. (2006) *Building Tomorrow's Talent.* Milton Keynes: AuthorHouse.

Michaels, E., Hadfield-Jones, H. and Axelrod, B. (2001) *The War for Talent.* Boston, MA: Harvard Business School Press.

NCSL (2008) *Review of the Landscape: Leadership and Leadership Development.* Nottingham: NCSL.

Talent assessment framework: talent development

Rate yourself (in partnership discussion) on the following categories.

1 = not at all; 2 = only partially; 3 = to a degree; 4 = very often; 5 = completely

Values

Do your talent development processes effectively evaluate the skills needed for leaders to develop trust?	1 2 3 4 5
How important is it for your organisation to detect talent, rather than respond to the more forceful personalities?	1 2 3 4 5

Personal qualities

How well do you evaluate the emotional and social effectiveness of potential leaders?	1 2 3 4 5
Do staff feel they can openly discuss their developmental needs?	1 2 3 4 5

Working with others

How effectively do the stages of leadership inform your talent development programmes, pathways or processes?	1 2 3 4 5
Do your talent development processes effectively evaluate the skills needed for leaders to empower others?	1 2 3 4 5

Strategic acumen

What learning opportunities do you use which are effective to develop the personal and social behaviours of potential leaders?	1 2 3 4 5
How effectively do you develop the ability of potential leaders to align others with whole-school strategy?	1 2 3 4 5

Those items you have rated '1' or '2' would need to be developed while those ranked '4' or '5' need to be celebrated and sustained. Those rated '3' warrant further reflection.

Chapter 6

Professional learning

This chapter considers:

➤ a framework for learning skills, behaviours and opportunities
➤ leaders as lead learners
➤ the impact of leadership learning on a school
➤ learning opportunities to develop leadership potential
➤ developing a culture of leadership learning.

If talent is to be developed, it is vital that the organisation has a well-developed and effective professional learning culture. Why professional learning? This suggests a more positive stance, not just signifying that staff need improving but that learning is part of being professional, a positive aspect of living in a changing situation. A learner is engaged in the process, reflects on experiences, develops understanding, makes judgements and brings action for change. Effective professional learning involves a change in knowledge, skills, attitudes or values and should link to the needs of the organisation. Talented leaders need to be mindful of their own learning and have a real concern for the learning of others.

We have already established that a strategic leader needs to learn in order to support the development of the organisation. The strategic dimension of learning answers the following three questions:

➤ What are we doing?
➤ Why are we doing it?
➤ What comes next?

Most leaders start their professional journey by demonstrating technical excellence in their teaching or support role. As they travel towards leadership, they may not use their current technical expertise but will develop a mastery of other areas, such as personal proficiency, leading and managing people, developing and articulating values and strategic acumen. We have identified four stages of learning and matched behaviours and skills of these learning stages to possible professional learning opportunities.

	Learning skills	Learning behaviours	Learning opportunities
Stage 1 Concern for immediate, technical competency	Connect Experience Understand Listen	Learn from experiences Focus on individual work	Observation Coaching Shared planning Reflective reading group
Stage 2 Technical Mastery	Reflect Review Question	Develop credibility Share practice	International visits Action learning/research Collaborative learning projects Being coached
Stage 3 Learning Leading	Notice Consider Apply Analyse	Teach others Lead the team	Using identifiable shareable practice Peer observation Using evidence Research projects Coaching Reflective reading group
Stage 4 Leading Mastery	Evaluate Create	Stimulate others through ideas Influence others Provide responsible organisation direction	Reflective thinking Conference speaking Post-graduate accreditation

Figure 6.1 *Learning skills, behaviours and opportunities*

Effective leaders, and potential leaders, need to appreciate their role in fostering professional learning, for themselves and their colleagues. Adult learning is a process, where the learner is active, as well as an outcome. It is well accepted that learning is more likely to be effective if it is relevant to the learner, can link with what is already known and if it is interesting and useful. Potential leaders should both demonstrate some skill in Stage 3 (Figure 6.1) but also be given opportunities to move to Stage 4. Stage 3 is about trying yourself and finding out 'how is ... similar to ...?'. Stage 4 is about asking 'Could there have been a better solution?' It is about creativity and the development of ideas. The ability to evaluate and create are essential attributes of talented leaders.

Leaders need to be lead learners in order to lead learning

Taking responsibility for your own learning is an important part of leadership. It is important to think clearly about what you need as a leader and to be proactive in attaining it, in order to:

➤ help you to make realistic and truthful self-assessments
➤ see the possibilities of career choices
➤ see how you can use research and further study to develop under-standing
➤ discuss wider issues in education as well as your own practice
➤ increase job motivation and job satisfaction
➤ enable your participation in wider professional communities
➤ enable you to have the experience and skill to help your colleagues learn.

How you learn is possibly just as important as what you learn. Creating an effective professional learning community is vital, in order to integrate professional learning into the way a school operates. We believe that for maximum benefit, all members of staff should be involved – and the following characteristics are important:

➤ Values: shared values
➤ Strategic acumen: shared vision
➤ Personal qualities: an atmosphere of trust, respect and support
➤ Working with others: collaboration across networks and partnerships.

Increasingly, trust seems to be the foundation stone. Trust is important if staff are taking risks or experimenting with new ideas or practices. Leaders or potential leaders need to be trusted that learning through mistakes will be allowed. In looking at learning opportunities, there is a debate between providing opportunities which have an obvious benefit for the pupils and the school and providing opportunities which are important activities in their own right for the individual person. In our experience, if staff cannot answer 'What's in it for me?', the professional learning will not be effective, especially for talented staff.

The impact on the whole school

We have established that school leaders need to be the lead learner. Any model for any process is not a blueprint for other schools but acts as a framework for others in your school to reflect on their practice and to learn. It is important that any model is adapted to suit the context and the culture of your school. The importance of a school's values, for example how much trust, collaboration, openness and flexibility there is to enable staff to take responsibility for change, desire to improve own practice and support others, is vital. If these values are present in practice, not rhetoric, then concerns and issues are tackled on class and school levels which will lead to a more effective school community. One school describes it as follows.

Insight from practice: every staff member a leader of learning and change

Through our strategic process, all staff have been energised – through taking part in enquiry projects and taking part in professional discourse, they want to make a difference to our school. It is important to stress the importance of focusing on the 'internal conditions' which favour change. This has certainly been true for us – so far it has been a six-year journey where we have developed and embedded processes to support professional development and school improvement. This means that change is possible throughout our school, it is something we create rather than it being something which is done to us, and it is part of our community. It is the way we learn and evaluate our understanding. School improvement depends on the commitment and active involvement of staff and groups within our school. Our approach centres on the premise that it is the staff who are best placed to develop understanding and to use that understanding to inform change and improvement. We agree that every staff member is a change agent. Our approach is concerned with a framework to support the learning, motivation and job satisfaction of individual members of staff through their empowerment.

Many staff development initiatives take the form of dissemination to staff rather than staff working together to build understanding. Leaders therefore need to take seriously the whole member of staff, their purpose, that member of staff as a person and then take seriously the real context in which they work. All staff need a sense of ownership of their learning. People have to be at the centre to create a motivational environment. If we consider the level of self-motivation, together with a person's skill ability, it would help us to identify talented individuals. This balance of motivation and skill can be seen in Figure 6.2.

	Low ——— Motivation ——— High	
	Motivation high Skill set low **Developing learner**	Motivation high Skill set high **Inspired learner**
	Motivation low Skill set low **Non learner**	Motivation low Skill set high **Uninspired learner**
	Low **Skill Set** High	

Figure 6.2 *Balancing skills and motivation*

Staff need to be at the centre of school improvement. The strength of the school improvement paradigm is that school is at the centre of any change. The internal context and culture of the school are vital for successful school improvement. If staff are able to voice their own interpretations of what makes their school effective, then learning may be incorporated in the wider targets for improvement. The process of actively engaging staff in seeking the truth, for their unique context, is vital for sustained improvement and for developing talented individuals. Does your school have a culture which supports this approach? The following is a useful inventory to analyse this:

What is the staff learning culture in your school?

For each statement below, indicate how accurately the statement describes you.
1 indicates 'not at all' on a graded scale to 5 which indicates 'completely'.

1. Is there a collective commitment to your school's   1 2 3 4 5
   vision, strategic direction, values, ethos and philosophy?

2. Do staff work with each other in planning, curriculum   1 2 3 4 5
   development, resource preparation or action research?

3. Does your approach to professional learning rely on   1 2 3 4 5
   cooperative relationships and mutual respect?

4. Do staff collaborate because they believe in the value of 1 2 3 4 5
   joint working and sharing?

5. Do you believe that progress and achievement are the   1 2 3 4 5
   responsibility of everyone?

6. Do staff believe that we are all learners, that improvement 1 2 3 4 5
   is always possible and that the process is always more
   important than the end result?

7. Is there openness and the ability to express views and to listen 1 2 3 4 5
   to differing views?

8. Is there a willingness to take risks, to try something different? 1 2 3 4 5

9. Is there a readiness to celebrate with and for others' effort 1 2 3 4 5
   and success?

Enquiry and reflection are vital if a school is to be a learning organisation. Research helps us to understand and refine our practice. The value and significance of professional learning for one school in our research is demonstrated in the following insight:

Insight from practice: professional learning

We believe that professional learning is an entitlement and a responsibility for all staff. With access to a wide range of learning experiences, to deepen skills, abilities, values, knowledge and attitudes, investment in professional learning will ensure a learning community, where staff work together, learn from each other and share best practice. Our aim is:

> ➤ for each of us to get better at our jobs
> ➤ to develop the learning of our children
> ➤ to engage in the improvement of teaching and learning
> ➤ to motivate, support and value staff
> ➤ for staff to make a difference in our school.

Learning opportunities to develop leadership potential

We have already established that learning opportunities to develop leadership potential should focus on evaluation and creativity. Thorne and Pellant (2007) suggest that organisations should 'hire for attitude and train for whatever'. Processes should be able to identify individual needs and talents and enable leaders to map these to the roles possible in the organisation and identify possible development and support. When considering the development of talent, it is important to prioritise resources to potential, and to people who will make the most difference. It is important to consider how we create the right environment for talent to thrive. Essential to this process is to match how people learn with the needs of talented people and provide a range of varied practices to promote professional learning. For example, there needs to be recognition that sideways moves often present bigger challenges than moves up the hierarchy (Hay Group, 2005) and that any challenge should be highly personal – 'engagement can transform, align and motivate' (Cheese et al., 2008). Some of the practices that exist in the organisation for all staff may be more appropriate than others for talent development. The following is a list of potential professional learning activities:

• Mentor/mentoring	• School-based research project
• Coach/coaching	• Guided reading
• Individual work project	• Job rotation
• Sabbatical	• Work shadowing
• Honest observation/360°	• Action learning
• Higher qualification	• Course
• Teaching others	• International visits
• Educational writing	• Networking

Figure 6.3 *Types of professional learning*

The reader can now reflect on their own school and the degree to which they utilise different professional learning approaches in the following reflection point:

Reflection point:

Which professional learning activities from Figure 6.3 would you include in a personal development plan to develop an individual with talent?

We will focus our discussion on four approaches, as exemplars of good practice, which have been used very effectively in schools to develop potential leaders. These are:

➤ school-based research projects
➤ international visits
➤ school-based masters courses
➤ reflective reading groups.

School-based research projects

All the above activities, in Figure 6.3, involve the learner in finding something out through researching, experience, practice or concepts. It is generally recognised that for schools to become learning communities, then research plays a key role in development and improvement (Handscombe and MacBeath, 2003). Staff need the opportunity to influence the decision-making process. Sustained learning by staff increases job satisfaction and helps to create a learning culture. We believe that the learning process that staff go through mirrors the process we wish to engender in the pupils:

➤ curiosity
➤ research
➤ collaboration
➤ applied learning.

Reflection point

➤ What question about leading or learning do you want to explore?
➤ Why is that enquiry relevant to your school?
➤ How will you collect evidence?
➤ How will you check the interpretation of evidence?
➤ How will you share your learning?
➤ What are the implications for your school?
➤ What are the implications for your learning?

We asked a group of potential leaders what they needed in order to be successful with their research. They replied, having 'release time' and having 'staff to discuss their project with' but when considering what was critical to their success, they identified having 'a head teacher who supported and encouraged them'.

Potential leaders need to identify the wider benefits of their projects and should be able to answer the following questions:

➤ What were the main benefits of your research for:
  ➤ students?
  ➤ the researcher?
  ➤ others?
  ➤ the whole school?
➤ What have you learned?
➤ What advice would you give others undertaking similar projects?
➤ How has the involvement in the project made you more effective in your role?

Enhanced learning by pupils requires sustained learning by staff and schools and that in turn increases job satisfaction and helps create a learning culture in schools. In one school, teaching and support staff were involved in research projects – they expressed the effects on their own motivation as the recognition of what they achieved and how they achieved being very motivational.

In this school, from our research project, talented support staff were encouraged to become involved in research projects.

Insight from practice: research projects

I carried out a school-based research project to investigate the effect of role play on children's speaking skills. My findings revealed that well-planned, creative role play can generate almost continuous speech and interaction amongst the participants. The school recognised my findings and reinforced the use of role play across the school, providing a variety of role play options for the children. Personally, the research provided me with the confidence to be more creative in my own practice and to share ideas with my colleagues.

My research was published by the university where I studied. This was a great honour which made me feel very proud of my work. This achievement was highlighted in my workplace which made me feel valued and keen to use my abilities further.

International visits

Visits to other schools give excellent opportunities for professional learning and provide insights that other forms of continuing professional development cannot. New ideas are brought back to school and with reflection it is possible to develop a whole-school perspective. Individual staff have ownership of the idea or practice and are able to reflect on the effects of that practice in a different educational organisation or system. This is very significantly enhanced with visits overseas which challenge the cultural mindset of those involved. The member of staff is not only able to observe practice internationally but is able to define new ideas and a way forward for their own school. The following are examples of the impact on practice for a member of support staff and a member of the teaching staff.

Insight from practice: international visits 1

I was fortunate enough to be given the opportunity, after completing the Certificate of School Business Management and the Diploma in School Business Management, to visit two primary schools and a secondary school in Melbourne, Australia. During my visits, I gained a fantastic insight into how an experienced and well-trained School

Business Manager (SBM) can work alongside the head teacher as part of the School Leadership Team, managing and leading the day-to-day running of the school, allowing the head teacher to concentrate fully on leading the teaching and learning of pupils and staff.

Without visiting these schools, all of whom employ an SBM, I would not have fully appreciated what a positive role an effective and efficient SBM has within a school.

On a personal level I came away feeling extremely motivated and positive with regard to my own role and believe, because of this, I have been able to be more effective within my own school.

Insight from practice: international visits 2

I worked in an environment openly promoting opportunity and felt privileged to be able to visit four primary schools in Australia. I had a PSHE focus and was given the freedom to be led by what I encountered. The result was one of excitement, motivation and fresh ideas. Further developed reflection led me to new challenges and questions. While, at the time, I only saw this transforming my personal and classroom practice, two years on and in a different educational environment the benefits of my visit continue to be developed with others.

School-based masters courses

Long-term award-bearing courses are of considerable value to encourage a high level of reflection, critical analysis and evaluation. Participants demonstrate substantial personal and professional growth. This school decided to create a network and deliver the masters course as a school-based project in order to enable local discussion and systematic enquiry which would support the schools locally.

Insight from practice: school-based masters courses

The school-based masters course gave me the opportunity to develop my knowledge and skills in many ways. During action research modules, I researched, planned, led and evaluated a variety of projects linked to curriculum areas that interested me. These were also chosen to be of benefit to the school as they were linked to school improvement objectives. Outcomes included the establishment of a peer listening scheme which had a direct impact on children's behaviour.

The focus for one module was leadership and management theories and practice. I was able to analyse my preferred leadership style and identified key skills which I needed to develop. The school-based masters course was not something I would have considered working towards individually but welcomed the school support and network. It was a valuable experience for my development.

Training outside school often has a limited impact inside school. However, the training in the next 'insight from practice' led to improved practice throughout the school and the staff were able to influence effective practice beyond their team. Neither member of staff was in a leadership role, but both were identified with potential.

Insight from practice: internal and external training

We attended six days of visual literacy training over a period of nine months: two sessions in school and four out of school. The first session was an introduction to film literacy, story boards and building up film vocabulary. The second session was how to use digital cameras using play mobile figures. The third session was using a programme called '2animate'. In the final session, we gave a presentation of how we would use visual literacy in our school. The two sessions in school gave us the opportunity to practise what we had learnt.

We were asked to share our knowledge with the rest of the staff through leading a professional learning meeting where colleagues carried out various tasks and activities. Having never led a staff meeting, this was rather daunting but when we had finished we felt our confidence had grown.

This training example had given the two staff members new ideas and the opportunity to reflect on practice together. With support in school, they had the confidence to lead the initiative in school. The key to this being effective in terms of talent development was:

> ➤ the opportunity to reflect with a colleague
> ➤ support in school
> ➤ the opportunity to lead a project
> ➤ the opportunity to be creative
> ➤ the opportunity to feel valued and have an impact.

Self-evaluation is an increasingly important aspect of school life and it is used to improve practice, to prove practice and to learn about practice. Self-evaluation is about closing the gap between where your school is now and where you want to be, and action research is a process for transformational practice in professional learning.

It is important that organisations ensure that talented staff have opportunities for these activities. Reflective practice supports evidence-based evaluation of practice and professional learning. Much traditional academic research in education is not sufficiently concerned with practice-based research in schools. Handscombe and MacBeath (2003) propose that schools can become research engaged by placing research activity at the heart of professional learning practice; they suggest that a research-engaged school:

> ➤ has a research orientation
> ➤ has a research-rich pedagogy
> ➤ promotes research communities
> ➤ puts research at the heart of school policy and practice.

Essentially, staff question, investigate and reflect on practice in order to inform better practice. By reflecting on practice in a systematic way, new insights are gained and effective changes are made. The 'practice' could be related to leadership, pedagogy, curriculum or assessment, in fact any aspect of school life. Staff should meet regularly to discuss their findings and experiences which will enable and sustain learning conversations and promote reflection together.

Reflective reading groups

One of the most powerful ways of developing leadership understanding and practice is to engage in leadership reading groups. This can take a number of forms. Senior leadership teams can adopt a leadership book for the year and agree to read a chapter a month and discuss it in a one-hour one-issue meeting as a framework to review their practice. Leadership development groups can take themes such as school improvement or strategy and agree to share chapters and articles to build up a common understanding. Staff at department or key stage grouping can take a short two-page ideas piece and use that as a discussion point for one of their meetings. The effectiveness of these approaches depends on the reading being focused, not too long and one that stimulates interest and discussion. One of the schools that we have worked with relates an account of the leader giving out two sides of an A4-length article every half term for colleagues to read and discuss after the holiday break. Initial reactions were non-committal but after two years, staff started asking 'Where is the holiday reading?'. Reflective practice had become part of the culture. What follows is an example of reflective reading in action at one school.

Insight from practice: reflective reading groups

Our interest in using research started with our reading groups. The leadership team used chapters from *Essentials of School Leadership* (Davies, 2009) in order to reflect on our own practice. This led to improved behaviour and change in school practice. We formed an 'NQT plus one' group in order for young teachers to continue their thinking. They too had a chosen book or research paper which was read and discussed, for example *Essential Motivation in the Classroom* by Ian Gilbert (2002).

Effective school improvement depends on clarity of thinking and we believe that reading is essential to develop rigour. Every holiday, all staff were invited to read a chosen article or research evidence which was discussed in our first meeting of the term. Our head teacher also established a professional library of recent books which were relevant to our ongoing developments or which challenged our thinking. Initially, the head teacher and then the leadership team chose the reading material, but as we progressed teaching and support staff volunteered relevant readings for our school team. The focus on our own reading helped to raise awareness of issues and initiatives; it kept us informed about relevant research. The holiday reading encouraged us to want to read wider; this was supported through the ease of access of books in our school.

The discussions also led to changed practice, and the focus for shared research projects. Our research projects have been linked to school improvement and the improvement of learning and teaching. We were successful in gaining funding which enabled us to fund fees for some staff to work on higher qualifications. Being involved with colleagues from the universities of Hull and Sheffield Hallam gave us the expertise and academic understanding of being practitioner researchers. The more we did, the more other people wanted to be involved. Awareness of what we were doing encouraged us to actively think about how we could do this more effectively. Being involved in research and regular discussion with colleagues was motivational and as one member of staff said, 'it helped to make our school a great place to learn and work'.

In all these reflective reading group approaches, it is important to clarify the issue of concern and focus on the defined professional learning question. It is important that any research developed understanding and introduced change to areas which were perceived to need improvement. It is important to study the impact of change in order that positive change is shared. The benefits for potential leaders included:

➤ enhanced self-esteem
➤ increased belief in their ability to make a difference
➤ greater willingness to make changes
➤ greater confidence in making changes
➤ enhanced understanding.

The importance of culture

It is possible to look at the amount of motivation a person has in relation to the impact that person has in effecting change in others. Potential leaders need motivation and support. Figure 6.4, after Rhodes et al. (2005), demonstrates that self-motivated, well-supported potential leaders contribute to a culture of collaboration.

Without leadership support, any research undertaken by individuals will have limited effect, indeed completion of any project would be more difficult. From this model, we can see that in order to have any chance of sustaining research and realising potential benefits, an ethos of collaboration is essential. In our research, we observed that in schools where the leadership did not support or even 'see the point of the research', researchers were soon de-motivated and gave up. Staff needed support to change their learning to any effective school improvement. We observed that where staff felt empowered and involved in the decision-making process and were part of a team where learning is accepted, then school improvement was realised. In order for this to happen, leaders need the skills to:

> empower staff professional learning
> encourage the sharing of new insights
> evaluate a school-based project in order to secure improvement
> facilitate good communication.

Leadership support High → Low	**Atmosphere of telling** Low motivation Low impact	**Atmosphere of collaboration** High motivation High impact
	Atmosphere of unresponsiveness Low motivation No impact	**Atmosphere of individualism** High motivation Low impact
	Low **Staff commitment** High	

Figure 6.4 *Leadership support and staff commitment*

Empowerment involves staff being able to create improvement actions for themselves and to be aware of whole-school priorities but also to be able to conduct research which is meaningful for their practice. As Carter and Halsall (2001: 71) say, informed changes happen where staff are 'definers of their own reality through being able to investigate and reflect on self-chosen practices'. Our readers could now consider the reflection point opposite.

Reflection point

➢ Does your school culture support the development of talent?
➢ Is there a commitment to potential leadership development?
➢ Are the needs of the school integrated with staff needs?
➢ Is the leadership team committed to this approach and to fund finding?
➢ Is time created for reflection, dialogue and coaching?
➢ Do staff feel ownership of their professional learning?
➢ Do processes encourage participation and collaboration rather than cooperation?

Learning must have an impact

It is important to establish a clear focus for learning by considering what is already known and then identifying where you may find out more. It is important to refer to a knowledge base throughout the learning journey. This knowledge base could be literature or research findings or it could be data, which should be used to inform your practice or to inform the enquiry. It is important to link the reading of theoretical frameworks to your professional context, thus locating any enquiry within the paradigms of research and evaluation. It is about reflecting on and challenging practice through a theoretical frame. It is critical to tell the story of how findings can help practitioners rather than to tell the story of research findings. This process needs the promotion of a culture which is open to research through the provision of transformational learning opportunities. This involves working collaboratively, sharing practice, engaging in professional dialogue and reflecting on current practice through observation and feedback.

Figure 6.5 demonstrates the impact of leadership involvement in research and staff involvement in research on the climate of the school. A climate of openness and trust is supported by high staff and low leadership involvement in research. A climate of complacency is characterised by low staff and high leadership involvement.

Rogers (1995) identifies four key elements which are critical in determining whether and how new ideas can be successfully adopted and implemented:

➢ A determined focus on understanding the nature of innovation and an exploration of how people in the organisation understand it

> how effective the channels are for communication and for exchanging information on an ongoing basis as innovation beds down
> how realistic are the timescales and plans for moving forward
> what arrangements exist for the need for new knowledge and practice to be constructed collaboratively and whether social systems support joint problem solving.

High	**Climate of dislocation** Staff committed to research but act in isolation Little impact on whole school	**Climate of openness and trust** Staff committed to research and collaboration High impact on whole-school development
Low Staff involvement in research	**Climate of ineffectiveness** Staff indifferent to research No whole-school improvement	**Climate of complacency** Staff indifferent so led by control Little commitment or empowered whole-school improvement
	Low **Leadership involvement in research** High	

Figure 6.5 *The impact of research involvement on the school culture*

Schools should therefore link intervention to staff needs and staff-identified problems. They should establish effective internal and external networks and allocate time for information sharing and discussion. Arrangements should be made to ensure joint problem solving and planning. So much can be gained through this shared use of time, far more than just to reduce workload, in terms of good quality discussion, effective innovation and creative initiatives. A culture of trust and mutual respect is important in persuading staff and leaders to take the risks involved in reviewing and revising practice in the light of the research.

Lessons for effective professional learning

For effective leadership learning to take place in schools, it is worth considering a number of points:

- ➤ Learning takes time – give sufficient time to projects. There has been a tendency, under pressure from central government initiatives, to undertake too much too quickly. Learning needs to be both planned and carefully paced.
- ➤ It is important to facilitate collaboration – learning is most effective in groups or as a shared activity. The ability to be able to share your understanding with others and to draw on the perspectives of others helps to create deep understanding.
- ➤ Leaders and managers need to be researching too – leadership learning is not only for those aspiring to promotion and advancement. It is critical for those already in senior posts to effectively do their current job and successfully drive change in the future.
- ➤ Learning should be linked to real-life school challenges – learning is better when it is contextualised. Improving schools from within rather than by external dictat is most likely to lead to sustainable change, so that addressing issues and learning about them can be a profound motivation for effective learning.
- ➤ How you do something and why you do it is as important as what you do – a climate of trust and openness is necessary to build cooperation from individuals and groups. Learning should be a shared and collaborative activity if all the insights and resources are to be drawn on.
- ➤ Learning should take risks – if individuals take risks and learn from intelligent failure, then the organisation is more likely to improve than if it is afraid to change and develop or has a blame culture.
- ➤ Disseminating learning and good practice is the key to organisational improvement. Effective learning is not something that always comes from without the school. Very often, high-quality learning and insights exist within the school but they are not shared and disseminated. The 'so what?' question is important – so what will be the impact on the school or how will we disseminate it?

Conclusion

This chapter has considered the nature and dimensions of effective professional learning in school. The central concept of the need for the leader to be the lead learner cannot be overemphasised. The way that leaders model behaviours in this area is critical in creating a learning culture in the school. We would suggest that schools should move away from the traditional concept of staff development and move to professional learning approaches, pathways and culture.

Suggested further reading

Byham, W.C., Smith, A.B. and Paese, M.J. (2002) *Grow Your Own Leaders*. London: FT Press.
Davies, B. (2007) *Developing Sustainable Leadership*. London: Sage.
Davies, B. and Brundrett, M. (2010) *Developing Successful Leadership*. New York: Springer.
Thorne, K. and Pellant, D. (2007) *Everything You Ever Needed to Know about Training*. London: Kogan Page.

Talent assessment framework: professional learning

Rate yourself (in partnership discussion) on the following categories.

1 = not at all; 2 = only partially; 3 = to a degree; 4 = very often; 5 = completely

Values

Does your school culture support the development of talent?	1	2	3	4	5
Do all staff ask the question 'what have I learned today?', as well as considering what the children have learned?	1	2	3	4	5

Personal qualities

Do you use a consideration of motivation to identify talent?	1	2	3	4	5
Do all your leaders take responsibility for their own learning?	1	2	3	4	5

Working with others

How important is research in your process for developing talent?	1	2	3	4	5
How do you encourage your potential leaders to read and reflect?	1	2	3	4	5

Strategic acumen

How do you work towards creating a motivational environment?	1	2	3	4	5
Are you building a leadership pool for future appointments?	1	2	3	4	5

Those items you have rated '1' or '2' would need to be developed while those ranked '4' or '5' need to be celebrated and sustained. Those rated '3' warrant further reflection.

Chapter 7

The architecture to support talent development

This chapter considers:

➤ the architecture to support talent development
➤ the importance of leadership coaching
➤ primary and secondary examples of talent-development architecture.

We have established that talent management is the integration of talent identification with the development of talent. Identification is practised through the effective evaluation of performance and the ability to discriminate between performance and potential. Development is practised through the provision of appropriate learning opportunities to empower potential leaders. Identification and development involve alignment, collaboration and a value-driven culture. All of this practice involves pathways, programmes and processes, the totality of which we are calling the architecture to support the management of talent. The nature of these pathways, programmes and processes can be seen in Figure 7.1.

The importance of leadership coaching to support talent development

Many of the processes we have described are more effective if the potential leader is coached. Many of the pathways and programmes have more impact if the potential leader is coached. We could have included a commentary on coaching in many of the chapters but because it is fundamental to many aspects of the architecture, we include it here. Coaching needs to be provided for potential leaders but it is also a skill potential leaders need to develop.

Pathways	Programmes	Processes
The pathways are developmental moves which are designed to give potential leaders the necessary experiences, coaching and mentoring to develop their potential into outstanding performance.	Various developmental programmes are necessary which, depending on identified need, may focus on: • knowledge • skills • behaviours • attitudes. Potential leaders will also need to develop the personal qualities and wisdom needed to make judgements when working in ambiguous and uncertain situations.	These are the fundamental activities which together provide a consistent and comprehensive system for the development of leadership talent.

Figure 7.1 *The architecture of talent management*

Successful coaching is supported through:

➤ the culture of the school
➤ the knowledge and experience of leaders
➤ a range of opportunities for professional learning
➤ a willingness to share skills.

The following behaviours are fundamental for successful coaching:

➤ trust
➤ honesty
➤ respect
➤ openness
➤ empathy.

The quality of the relationship between the two participants is vital to the success of the coaching opportunity. Even the most robust system will not be successful if there is no trust between the potential leader and the coach. The following skills are essential for successful coaching:

➤ active and focused listening
➤ the ability to reflect and learn from experiences
➤ appropriate questioning
➤ recognition of feelings
➤ negotiation
➤ the ability to review the discussion

➤ the ability to challenge and confront
➤ the ability to evaluate observations.

In our experience, the ability to actively listen and the ability to ask appropriate questions are key skills which effective schools encourage all staff to develop. As well as being key to the coaching process, they are key to an effective performance-management process, both for the reviewer and the reviewee and for a mentoring process. One school used the following activity (insight from practice) with staff to practise active listening skills.

Insight from practice: developing listening skills

Staff worked in groups of three. The three roles to be undertaken in the exercise were discussed with everyone and the need for confidentiality and the following essential skills were agreed on:

Skills needed by the person being listened to (the storyteller)
➤ the ability to ask for help or advice
➤ the skill of self-evaluation
➤ the ability to express difficulties and strengths
➤ the ability to discuss needs, values and feelings.

Skills needed by the listener
➤ the ability to listen with attention
➤ the ability to give support and encouragement
➤ the skills of communicating respect, empathy and warmth.

Skills needed by the observer
➤ the ability to listen attentively
➤ the ability to distance self from the interview to achieve a more objective understanding
➤ the ability to give feedback in ways which encourage rather than threaten others.

The task took part in three sessions, each lasting 15 minutes. This ensured that everyone had the opportunity to undertake each role. The listening interview lasted for 10 minutes. Throughout the discussion, the observer was aware of the verbal and non-verbal aspects of both the storyteller's and listener's behaviours. The five-minute feedback session was led by the observer, but included discussion of how the feedback was received.

The groups were given the following information for the task.

(Continues)

(Continued)

Task 1

In groups of three, decide who will take each role for each session.

	Session 1	Session 2	Session 3
Storyteller			
Listener			
Observer			

The agenda for each storyteller and listener will be:

1. What aspects of your work have given you the greatest satisfaction over the past year?

    Include why you have been pleased with these areas of performance and what strengths and skills you have which could be used to greater advantage.

2. What aspects of your work have not gone as well as you would have hoped?

    Identify any obstacles that prevented success and whether anything could have been done to support you. Include how you would like to improve those areas of your performance.

The observer used the following record sheet.

	Helpful behaviour	Unhelpful behaviour
Beginning the discussion ➢ Seating arrangements ➢ Putting the storyteller at ease ➢ Posture, gestures, smiles		
During the discussion ➢ Expressing interest ➢ Use of open-ended questions ➢ Paraphrasing for clarification ➢ Maintaining momentum and use of prompts ➢ Coping with silence		
Concluding the discussion ➢ Checking perceptions ➢ Summarising ➢ Helping the storyteller to feel positive ➢ Finishing off		

> **Task 2**
> Discuss how useful Task 1 has been in terms of developing skills and what should now be our way forward.

Communication skills are vital for many processes in school to be effective.

Effective listeners are able to:

➤ focus the discussion
➤ use verbal prompts
➤ ask questions to clarify meaning
➤ paraphrase to further the discussion
➤ summarise.

Effective questioners are able to ask questions in order:

➤ to elicit as much information as possible
  ➤ How would you describe your experience of ...?
  ➤ What is the best way to take this forward?
  ➤ What are the advantages of ...?

➤ to investigate further
  ➤ How did you feel when ...?
  ➤ What makes that more difficult?
  ➤ Why is that important for you?

➤ to check out understanding
  ➤ Are you saying that ...?
  ➤ Would I be right in saying ...?

The following reflection point enables the reader to consider the effectiveness of a coaching event.

Reflection point

Think of a time when you have participated in a coaching session. Use the following prompts to help you to reflect on how effective this was for both of the participants.

➤ What behaviours make you judge the session as effective coaching?

(Continues)

(Continued)
- ➤ What types of questions were asked?
- ➤ Were any questions obstacles to effective coaching?
- ➤ How well did the coach listen to the views of the person being coached?
- ➤ How could you tell that active listening took place?
- ➤ Were there any behaviours which acted as obstacles to effective listening?
- ➤ How well did the participants work together to achieve solutions?
- ➤ How well did the coach summarise the discussion?
- ➤ How well did the participants reach an agreement on the best way forward?

With an effective talent development architecture, schools can reduce turnover of high-performing staff and manage their leadership succession planning. Effective processes, programmes and pathways need to be established. In this chapter, we are considering how schools could set up the architectures for identifying talent, recording talent development and outlining future needs from an organisational and an individual perspective. In order to do this, we need to put the talent architecture within the wider school context. It is vital that a school is able to:

Identify key strategic and operational targets

⬇

Articulate critical staffing implications

⬇

Identify talent demands

⬇

Evaluate talent availability

⬇

Develop a talent pool

⬇

Deploy talent to leadership roles and challenges

While the above model provides a theoretical and conceptual framework, we need to consider how schools operationalise this into a practical process for the evaluation and development of staff. We have included two insights from practice, one from the secondary phase and one from the primary phase. These schools have worked hard to set up a rational talent development framework for their organisations.

What each of these schools is seeking to achieve is a talent-management process which can:

1. Produce tangible evidence (data) that satisfies the need for a coherent, personal and organisational development programme.
2. Create engagement and 'buy in' from governors, senior management, teaching staff and support staff.
3. Link the talent-management process with existing performance management and development activities including role profiles and competency models.
4. Be flexible enough to accommodate the feedback from leaders and at the same time maintain the 'integrity' and 'fairness' of the evaluation processes.
5. Take account of the fast-changing challenges in school and participation in new and flexible ways of working.

We will now look at a secondary example of good practice.

Insight from practice: secondary school example

A group of schools are part of a Trust which has set up a coordinated and integrated talent management system. The Trust sees talent management as a much more sophisticated and important approach to developing talent than simple succession planning. It believes that effective leadership is at the heart of creating world-class learners and outcomes and is underpinned by a climate of trust. In order to embed leadership throughout the organisation and secure able and talented leaders for the future, the Trust is working to actively encourage and develop leadership talent.

Staff identified through our two-stage talent-management programme will be offered two leadership routes – one to become a 'Leader of Pedagogy' and the other to enable them to develop as 'Leaders of Organisations'. These routes will be joined by a set of common development opportunities including: access to masters qualifications, in-house leadership programmes, action-based research, shared leadership activities, etc. This programme is supported by ongoing coaching to allow individuals to develop expertise and, if required, change routes mid-flow.

(Continues)

(Continued)

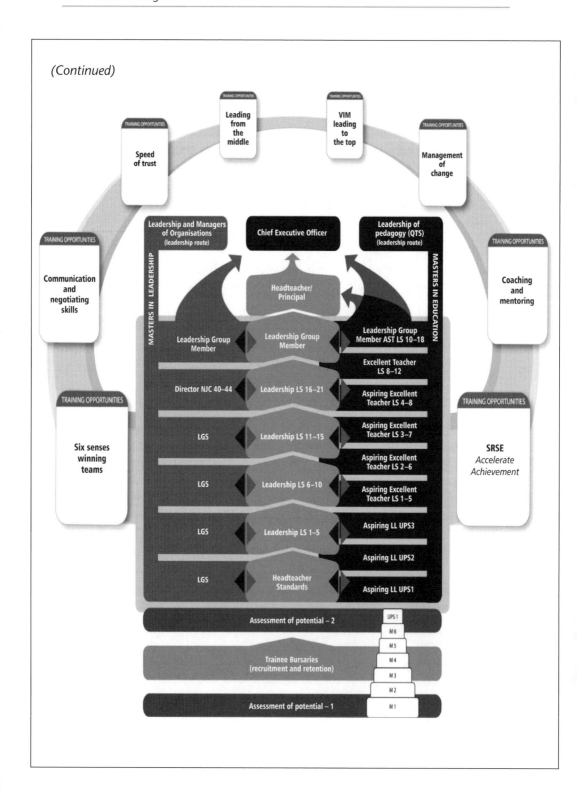

Process

Assessment of potential 1

Current performance of teaching staff is evaluated annually through analysis of the following criteria:

- ➤ cumulative lesson observation scores
- ➤ average value-added scores from teaching classes
- ➤ self-assessment (through PM) against Trust teacher/National Occupational Standards for support staff via *accelerate achievement*
- ➤ line manager assessment (as above).

The final score will be judged as red, amber or green and further weighted by national and local shortage subject areas (for teaching staff). Of course, current performance is not a reliable indicator of future potential, especially not in terms of leadership potential, therefore this is why the objective data is supported by the completion of both a self-assessment and the line manager's assessment of the individual – together, these identify the talent to be 'managed'.

Assessment of potential 2

Once 'talent' has been identified, individuals are then invited to complete a self audit and 360° assessments against the Trust Developing Leaders framework. This framework has been developed by combining elements from the NPQH, AST and Excellent Teacher standards, together with some input from industries outside of the education sector. Its design is in line with both the Trust vision 'to help students achieve world class learning outcomes by developing world class teachers in a world class community' and the belief that leaders are fundamental in creating a working climate in which all individuals can excel, contribute and share in this vision. Questions therefore focus on four key activities:

1. Developing trust
2. Setting standards and delivering world-class outcomes
3. Developing self and ensuring continuous development
4. Working with others and building high-performance teams.

The assessment itself uses a bespoke online tool which allows individuals and nominated representatives to assess against a set of detailed criteria on a 1–4 scale and store evidence to support these judgements:

(Continues)

(Continued)

1. Basic
2. Developing
3. Established
4. Extending.

Once the 360° assessment has been completed, we have a profile and set of evidence, against which to judge potential and identify development/training priorities. In order to get the most out of high potential staff, research suggests that individuals need and value ongoing feedback on progress, support from a coach, a clear development plan and time for reflection. The Trust therefore decides on a suitable coach for all staff on the leadership development programme and works through a clearly defined cycle:

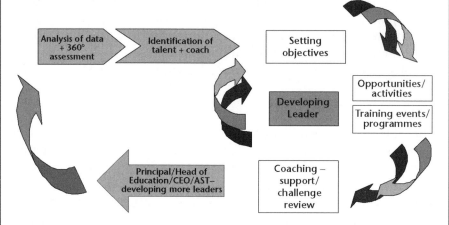

Development activities and training opportunities

In discussion with the coach, individuals design a programme of activities, tasks and training sessions to support and develop their leadership capabilities, selecting from:

➤ e-learning opportunities
➤ action-based research
➤ networking/job/role shadowing
➤ directed reading
➤ reflective writing
➤ masters modules:
  ➤ mentoring and coaching
  ➤ leading change
  ➤ building high-performance teams.

In line with the initial design of the Developing Leaders framework and to provide ongoing support for future applications for both NPQH, AST and Excellent Teacher status, these opportunities are clearly mapped against the standards, for example:

National standards for head teachers	Training/ development opps	Behaviours	Measures	Excellent teacher/AST standards
3. Developing self and working with others Effective relationships and communication are important in headship as head teachers work with and through others. Effective head teachers manage themselves and their relationships well. Headship is about building a professional learning community which enables others to achieve. Through performance management and effective continuing professional development practice, the head teacher supports all staff to achieve high standards. To equip themselves with the capacity to deal with the complexity of the role and the range of leadership skills and actions required of them, head teachers should be committed to their own continuing professional development.	**Performance management** Lesson observation training – Ofsted	Manages accountability	PM review, objectives etc. completed and agreed for team Review of lesson observation feedback	**Team working and collaboration** E14 Contribute to the professional development of colleagues using a broad range of techniques and skills appropriate to their needs so that they demonstrate enhanced and effective practice
	The art of delegation • delegation – the process • dos and don'ts	Delegates appropriately Communicates in a clear, consistent and open manner	ITT/NQT mentored successfully to meet Q/C standards	
	How to lead CPD (including induction, NQT and ITT)	Develops successful teams Presents confidently	CPD programme/ session designed and presented	
	Six senses – winning teams • why teams are successful (or not) • building trust and commitment • dealing with conflict • setting goals and objectives	Develops successful teams Builds effective relationships Works collaboratively Communicates in a clear, consistent and open manner	Departmental/faculty meetings chaired, minuted and actioned	**Planning** E7 (a) Take a lead in planning collaboratively with colleagues in order to promote effective practice (b) identify and explore links within and between subjects/curriculum areas in their planning
	Mentoring and coaching (Masters)	Developing others Builds effective relationships		
	Communication – getting it right • giving feedback with style • running effective meetings • non-verbal behaviour • lesson observation training – Ofsted	Communicates in a clear, consistent and open manner Practises accountability	Lesson observation and feedback completed as part of internal evaluation	**Team working and collaboration** E15 Make well-founded appraisals of situations upon which they are asked to advise, applying high level skills in classroom observation to evaluate and advise colleagues on their work and devising and implementing effective strategies to meet the learning needs of children and young people leading to improvements in pupil outcomes

Managing talent at organisational level

At Trust level, using the online assessment tool makes it possible to map job roles against the criteria, identifying the level of competence required for each leadership role. Once the database has analysed the results of the self-assessment and 360° audits, it is then possible to identify those individuals whose profile most closely meets the requirements for specific leadership roles as well as allowing individuals to plan their training programme to prepare them for chosen career pathways.

We now move on to a primary example of good practice.

Insight from practice: primary school example

We are a large primary school in the East Midlands. It is difficult to decide where the process for talent management begins, since it involves many school processes. However, the logical place to begin this description is with the identification of what we need. This is part of our strategic plan and the review of the leadership model has involved support staff, teaching staff and governors. The review was prompted by our desire to:

➤ continue to improve pupil learning
➤ involve support staff in positions of leadership
➤ create opportunities for the development of potential leaders
➤ find creative solutions.

We created the following model which was supported by descriptions of the behaviours needed to undertake each role:

	Deputy head FS–KS1	Deputy head KS2	Leading teacher	Leading teacher	Head teacher
Learning and teaching	SEN Gifted and talented Role model	Maths Enrichment activities Role model	English Assessment	Developing approaches to learning Creativity	Lead learning and teaching Learning Habits
Working with others	1:1 TAs Team TAs Induction Team Supply Parental workshops	Team TAs Induction Team Supply Parental workshops	Lead practice and development of responsibilities	Lead practice and development of responsibilities	Governors Parents' evenings Support staff School leadership team
Securing accountability	Standards FS Standards KS1 Curriculum planning SATs KS1 FS profile	Standards KS2 Curriculum planning Cross-curricular links SATs KS2	Standards English Cross-curricular links Assessment	Achievements Creativity	Monitoring and evaluation processes Performance management policies School data
Leading and managing	Events and duties KS1 Events and duties FS Assessment of, as and for Core Take-home tasks	Events and duties KS2 Assessment of, as and for Core School council Take-home tasks	Assessment of, as and for Foundation subjects	Assessment of, as and for Foundation subjects	Strategy/SIP Finance PPA SLT CPD research and development CPD, INSET, weekly profess-ional learning
Strengthening community through collaboration	External agencies KS1 work experience Looked after children	KS2 work experience Child protection Business enterprise	School visits Local community	Local community	Networks: International Local schools University Student teachers
Creating the future	Innovate to enhance learning Lead SIP action	Innovate to enhance learning Lead SIP action	Innovate to enhance learning	Innovate to enhance learning	Strategy Vision Values Research projects
ECM	Enjoy and achieve	Stay safe	Achieve economic well-being	Be healthy	Make a positive contribution
SMSC	Social	Moral	Cultural		Spiritual

Once we knew what we needed from the leadership team, we were able to recruit staff to the new positions. The behaviour descriptions helped us to evaluate potential leaders and identify the skills and behaviours to be developed in developing leaders and established leaders. We established a regular review system for these leadership descriptions to ensure we were solution focused.

The descriptors were used in our well-established and effective performance management process, both for self-evaluation and performance evaluation. All the evidence from these processes was discussed by the leadership team to ensure collaborative identification of potential leaders. This made us all aware of whether judgements and discussions were informed and open. All evaluations were used in feedback to staff. Sometimes our identification of leadership potential came as a shock to colleagues lacking in self-confidence. The support process was most valuable in those cases – each member of staff had a personal mentor and in addition, a coach would be chosen to support colleagues on their leadership journey. More problematic were situations where colleagues believed in their own leadership potential but hadn't demonstrated the required behaviours or skills. In this case, learning processes were aimed at key descriptors and supported opportunities clearly defined with agreed targets and outcomes. Mostly, these colleagues demonstrated a lack of personal skills which didn't help them then accept the judgements of others.

The new model was motivational and gave us the opportunity to target individual learning opportunities more specifically. Our professional learning process was well established and linked with our school strategic plan. We had good networks and were able to secure funding to enable many staff to take leadership learning opportunities. This was a key element in attracting high-quality applicants to our posts.

The annual professional review became an effective addition to our performance review process. It was voluntary but always taken up by those who identified themselves as potential leaders, as well as those who wanted to review their career options. The outcomes of these reviews always fed into our professional learning programme. The agenda included discussion of:

➤ career progression
➤ teaching experiences requested
➤ leadership opportunities requested
➤ professional learning requested at performance management review
➤ how the school could support a career progression.

(Continues)

(Continued)

Another key process was our cycle of gathering staff views, which involved an annual look at key processes and led to positive improvements. Staff were invited to identify which staff team they were part of: teaching, support, midday, site, administration. Sometimes specific questions were used, for example when asking staff their views about the leadership and management in the school and at other times a general profoma was used, for example:

Staff views 2010: School Improvement Planning, Professional Learning and Performance Management processes

	What do we do well?	What else could we do?
1. School improvement planning process		
2. Professional learning process		
3. Performance management process		
4. How well do we link these processes?		

Please rate each process where 1 is outstanding and 4 is ineffective

SIP				PL				PM				Linked processes			
1	2	3	4	1	2	3	4	1	2	3	4	1	2	3	4
Any other comments?															

Gathering views was part of our whole-school evaluation overview which followed a three-year cycle, and each year we focused on a different aspect.

Our school focus on leadership skills and behaviours was effective and well supported by learning opportunities, out-of-class reflection time, guided reflective reading and coaching.

These processes led to us recruiting excellent potential leaders and enabled established leaders to continue to learn and develop. However, one school is unable to create opportunities for potential leaders to advance in leadership positions, hence we were creating effective leaders only to lose them. Our talent-management programme certainly helped our successful appointment of middle-leader positions, and new leaders continued to be supported throughout the role.

Both of these insights from practice provide the structure and processes to develop an excellent architecture for talent development. These two schools have moved from the idea that 'talent development is a good concept' to a proactive delivery of talent development through the establishment of a robust architecture to support talent development.

Suggested further reading

Higham, R., Hopkins, D. and Matthews, P. (2009) *Systems Leadership in Practice*. Maidenhead: Open University Press.

Hopkins, D. (2007) *Every School a Great School*. Buckingham: Open University Press.

Jackson, M.C. (2003) *Systems Thinking: Creative Holism for Managers*. Chichester: John Wiley.

Talent assessment framework: architecture to support learning

Rate yourself (in partnership discussion) on the following categories.

1 = not at all; 2 = only partially; 3 = to a degree; 4 = very often; 5 = completely

Values

How well are the following values seen in practice in your school?

Trust	1 2 3 4 5
Honesty	1 2 3 4 5
Respect	1 2 3 4 5

Personal qualities

What pathways, programmes and processes do you have to support the development of a potential leader's personal qualities?	1 2 3 4 5
Is coaching available to all talented members of staff?	1 2 3 4 5

Working with others

What pathways, programmes and processes do you have to support the development of a potential leader working with others?	1 2 3 4 5
Does the quality of relationships enhance the processes for talent development in your school?	1 2 3 4 5

Strategic acumen

What pathways, programmes and processes do you have to support the development of a potential leader's strategic acumen?	1 2 3 4 5
Have you put talent architecture into the wider school context?	1 2 3 4 5

Those items you have rated '1' or '2' would need to be developed while those ranked '4' or '5' need to be celebrated and sustained. Those rated '3' warrant further reflection.

Section 3

Talent Culture

Chapter 8

Building a talent-management culture

This chapter considers:

➤ what culture is
➤ creating a positive leadership development culture
➤ insights from practice
➤ becoming a talent developer and engager.

What is culture?

The standard definition of culture is 'the way we do things around here'. Creating a talent culture or a talent development culture must be built on a positive organisational culture. If the school is going to be one that has a culture which rewards and enhances talented individuals, it should have a culture that is positive in its own right, it should be a place where people want to work and where they want to share their ideas and professional learning. Culture is about values, about shared beliefs, about purpose and about relationships. Our model for the dimensions of leadership (see Chapter 1) also identifies the important aspects for developing an effective culture for talent development – a culture where the values of trust and respect are at the heart of the organisation and seen in action, not just in rhetorical statements, a culture where teamwork and a sense of community thrive, where there is a common purpose and shared direction and where support and caring are the bedrock of sustainable success.

Effective leaders have learned to view their school's environment holistically, considering all factors. Using this wide-angle lens approach is what the concept of a school culture is all about. Thinking about the nature of culture gives leaders a broader framework for developing an understanding of the complexity of the organisation. We would argue that if leaders had a deeper understanding of the culture of their organisation, they would be better able to influence the values, beliefs and attitudes that are needed to create a nurturing and secure learning environment. 'Culture' has a wide variety of meanings, for example in horticulture it refers to a process of growth and development. The term 'culture' is often used in education as meaning the same as 'climate' or 'ethos', and for most definitions culture represents a pattern of meaning. These patterns of meaning are expressed explicitly through symbols and implicitly through taken-for-granted beliefs. Culture is formed over the course of a school's history, and is held in the shared values, beliefs and traditions of the school community. In the world of education, the culture focuses more on the core values needed to build a secure learning environment. This system of meaning often shapes what people think and how they behave in that organisation. It is a social condition, a way of life. A strong culture has been shown to correlate with improved student and staff achievements, motivation and satisfaction. Hence, a school is best able to improve if it has a clear and shared purpose, shared values and an effective organisational philosophy.

Deal and Peterson (1999), in an outstanding discussion of the role that leaders have in developing a positive organisational culture, outline a number of activities. The first two roles are focused on establishing the present culture of the school:

> The leader should be an 'historian' in order to understand the social and organisational past of the school. For example, it is important for a leader to know if staff have a positive mindset and have a positive view of their relationship with children, or if staff have a negative view and think that the lack of their success is due to the fact that 'now they send us the wrong sort of children'.
> The leader should also be an 'anthropological sleuth' who can analyse and probe to establish the current set of norms, values and beliefs which define the current culture.

Deal and Peterson then move on to consider the leadership roles which will help to move the culture forward:

> The leader as a 'visionary' who works with other leaders and the community to define a deeply value-focused picture for the school.
> The leader as a 'potter' who shapes and is shaped by the school's heroes, rituals, traditions, ceremonies and symbols and who brings in staff who share their core values.

It is clear from this discussion and from our experiences that the leader's role in understanding and developing the culture is vital. Deal and Peterson (1999: 116) outline what they consider as elements of a positive, successful culture as follows:

> a mission focused on student and teacher learning
> a rich sense of history and purpose
> core values of collegiality, performance and improvement that engender quality, achievement and learning for everyone
> positive beliefs and assumptions about the potential of students and staff to learn and grow
> a strong professional community that uses knowledge, experience and research to improve practice
> an informal network that fosters positive communication flow
> shared leadership that balances continuity and improvement
> rituals and ceremonies that reinforce core cultural values
> stories that celebrate successes and recognise heroines and heroes
> a physical environment that symbolises joy and pride
> a widely shared sense of respect and caring for everyone.

Leaders who perceive the need for change in the school's culture should therefore first understand the nature of culture, recognising that the beliefs, values or attitudes are at the very heart of the school's stability. Any change should be approached with meaningful dialogue and a great concern for others. As one of the leaders in our research commented: 'you don't know what you don't know – unearthing all the history of what has gone on and why people think as they do takes time and is very complicated'. Then leaders should understand the existing culture. The culture of the school has huge impact on everything undertaken; it could be said that it is the most influential aspect of any change and therefore leaders ignore it at their peril. However, it is also the most difficult aspect to change. The most effective change in school culture happens when leaders, staff and students behave in a way which models the shared values and beliefs. A leader who acts with care for and trust of others is more likely to develop a school culture with similar values. A leader who has little time for others, whatever the school value statement says, demonstrates that selfish behaviours and attitudes are acceptable. It is important that there is clarification of those values and beliefs so that the consequences of any change are considered and actively chosen if they have a positive impact. Leaders should nurture behaviours, traditions, celebrations, rituals and symbols which express and reinforce the effective school culture. Indeed, in new schools one of the tasks is to create the tradition.

Schools which reflect the positive cultural values outlined by Deal and Peterson (1999) at a whole-school level set the background for a positive leadership culture and, most significantly, a positive leadership development culture. One of the key questions for staff is: would they recommend a good friend to work at the school? Or to ask them whether they are proud to be associated with the school and its culture and values. We can also learn from the aspects and behaviours which produce a negative culture. Deal and Peterson (1999: 118) contrast these positive factors with elements of 'toxic' cultures:

➤ there is a focus on negative values
➤ staff cohesion is fractured; meaning is derived from subculture membership, anti-student sentiments or life outside work
➤ conversations are mutually destructive with in-fighting and negative group behaviour
➤ few positive relationships exist among adults, making positive relationships with students difficult.

The culture of being open or closed to new ideas, and being aware or unaware of major educational and economic developments, is a key one to enable or not enable talent to develop. This is amusingly represented by Robertson and Abbey (2001) who depict individuals in an organisation as follows:

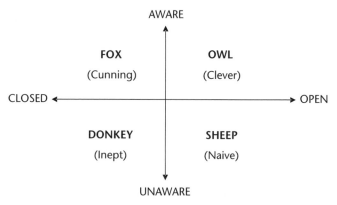

Figure 8.1 *People in organisations (Robertson and Abbey, 2001: 127),* Clued Up: Working Through Politics and Complexity, *Pearson Education Limited*

The sheep are newcomers who are open-minded and enthusiastic and they potentially offer a great deal to the school. However, they do not know the history of the school or its culture and therefore in the short term they can be naive in their understanding of the various individuals and relationships. Most significantly, they need to be protected from the 'toxic' members of staff who we call the foxes. These are individuals who are very aware of the history and the politics of the school but are closed-minded to change and development. They are clever and cynical and look for new staff to influence them to their point of view. Leaders need to isolate the foxes. The donkeys are hard working but have lost their way. They simply come in and do their job and make little wider school contribution. Leaders need to re-energise these staff. Owls are not uncritical but are realistic and will 'give new ideas a go'; they are positive and supportive. Leaders need to treasure the owls and help them to spread their influence. Amusingly, it might be said that the aim of talent-focused schools is to develop more owls, cull the foxes and develop the rest. It might be a useful exercise for the reader to consider if any of these creature types are on your staff and significantly what your plans are for them.

We need to consider what we can draw from these factors which will allow us to focus on developing positive leadership roles and positive leadership development frameworks to enable leadership talent to develop and grow. We all know schools or have worked in them where the culture is one of moaning or complaining and the language is one of 'battling' these attitudes which wear down staff enthusiasm and motivation. As leaders, we need to confront and tackle these cultures to a point where 'together we can' becomes the culture of the staff and 'all children can achieve and will achieve' becomes the value for the educational process. The challenge is one that has to be addressed with the realisation that it takes time to build new and positive cultures to replace negative and de-motivating ones. Now would be a useful point to review your organisation's culture by undertaking the following evaluation:

Evaluation exercise: thinking about the culture of your organisation

How well do the following statements reflect the leadership culture of your organisation?

A We excel at this
B We do this to a degree but have room for development
C This only happens in some areas of the organisation
D We are not very good at this

1. We put children and the school first above our personal interests	A B C D
2. Staff work collaboratively and work effectively as a team	A B C D
3. Staff welcome new ideas and discuss them positively	A B C D
4. We celebrate and take pride in others' successes	A B C D

5. We believe that we can always improve	A B C D
6. We have a 'no-blame culture' and learn from our mistakes	A B C D
7. We seek evidence on which to make decisions	A B C D
8. Leaders ask questions and seek ideas rather than impose their views	A B C D

In undertaking the evaluation exercise, you will have identified some areas for celebration and some areas for further thought or development which could be part of your action plan to improve the culture of the school. It may be worth considering what other colleagues in school feel and how they would rate the questions. Is your view shared? Building on this consideration of culture in general, we will now look specifically at creating and developing a 'talent culture' in schools, since an effective culture is essential to attract and retain the best talent.

Creating a positive leadership talent-development culture

The culture of an organisation determines how the people of that organisation perceive what is possible, how they assess risk and opportunity and what behaviour is appropriate. Enabling talent is a future-focused activity which facilitates the securing and enhancing of key staff. Loyalty, commitment and retention cannot be guaranteed but in the process of developing people to 'step up', organisations should ensure they encourage people to 'stay on board' and commit to the school's development. Talented people need to feel valued and to feel that their contribution is making a difference. One leader in our research said 'the reason I became a head was that when I was a deputy my head believed in me and my potential. It makes a huge difference when someone wants you to succeed'. Affirmation is powerful; feeling appreciated, recognised and being valued is motivational. Opportunities will help the talented person feel motivated and aligned to the organisation. Future opportunities and roles will also need to be available at the right time. Being part of a wider organisational group could help to make this happen. Cheese et al. (2008) express the view that motivation, commitment, trust, empathy and inspiration ensure that an individual is able to align their own interests with the organisation. When we consider the management of talent, we have considered three elements:

➢ identification
➢ development, which includes 'on-boarding' the induction into a new role, learning and coaching to improve performance in that role
➢ talent culture.

The culture of the school affects the way identification and development are practised and understood and affects what processes are in place for the identification and development of potential leaders. Our readers can now reflect on their own school:

Reflection point: thinking about engaging talent

Do you have processes which enable the talented individual to answer:

> What do I do really well?
> What would I like to do better?
> Who listens and will inspire me to achieve my ambition?
> What opportunities will help me realise my aspirations for advancement?

In becoming a talent-focused organisation, it is important to consider what factors help you to be described as 'employer of choice'. These factors may help a talented person be excited by their work and their working environment which will therefore help the organisation to retain those talented people who otherwise may move for the offer of better rewards or better support in a different organisation. The organisation should:

> be committed for the long term
> be relentlessly reflective and striving for continuous improvement
> have a culture based on shared values and beliefs
> be engaged with the hearts and minds of individuals
> give positive feedback and show an interest in new ideas and development
> support a curiosity to learn and to change.

Changing the culture can't be a quick fix; it takes a long time because the culture is changed and developed through people's beliefs and behaviours. It is changed through actions rather than through articulation alone. Certain prerequisites can be identified in the establishment of a talent culture.

1. Seek commitment from all leaders

All leaders, at all levels, must demonstrate their support for implementing a talent mindset. It is very important that this is done by the whole organisation and not just by the head teacher. Across the school in leadership teams and most significantly from the middle leadership team, there needs to be a culture of appointing great staff and developing them so those staff outgrow current roles and are ready for new challenges. It is not always easy for established middle leaders to have new and challenging staff working with them, especially if the new and challenging staff are more talented than them. Middle leaders should see themselves as mentors or coaches and not blockers to new talent. The contribution a leader makes to developing leaders within their school should be part of the focus for middle and senior leaders' performance-management process.

2. Define what good leadership is

The national school inspection process has encouraged the evaluation of what the quality of teaching looks like in schools. The standards for effective teaching are well documented and understood and used by schools and teachers in order to describe the quality of teaching. Leaders in schools regularly observe and analyse the quality of teaching and the effectiveness of teachers. It is apparent from our research that similarly clear definitions of the nature and dimensions of leadership at middle and senior levels are not articulated nor documented to anything like the same degree. The quality of leadership and the effectiveness of leaders are not regularly evaluated and analysed by schools. Schools need to determine and describe the skills, abilities and effective behaviours of their leaders and have the means of evaluating them.

3. Use multiple methods for judging leadership potential and development

Evidence needs to be assembled to provide leadership profiles for staff in order to evaluate the suitability of a potential leader for a post and for them to demonstrate their competency. A variety of methods can be used to achieve this, such as the outcomes from 360-degree reviews, analysis from coaching activities and the impact from 'in-house' learning provision. The aim of using multiple methods is to provide the developing leader with insights and perspectives that they can draw on to focus on their own learning needs and give them the support to act on the information.

4. Formulate future strategic objectives and align with talent development

It is important to take a positive approach to talent management and not to 'bolt on' a talent-management approach to other school leadership and management activities. Talent management needs to be set within the strategic priorities of the school and the development of talent needs to clearly fit with both the organisational culture and the organisational purpose. 'What we want to do' and 'how we want to act' need to be clearly established so that leaders can answer the question of 'who they want' to fit in with their culture and help them to reach their purpose.

We have established that what the organisation stands for is often the focus when we consider culture. In the business world, this is sometimes called the 'brand'. A brand can be more than a product – it is more often a symbol of service and the way staff in the organisation treat each other and their customers. The way staff work and the values they hold become part of the brand. Thus, customers will see a difference in the brand when it comes to the values of service and the approach to customer relations that, for example, British Airways or Singapore Airlines demonstrate through their actions. There is much simplistic criticism within the educational academic community of using such business terms as 'brand'. This is often misplaced as all that a 'brand' or 'what we stand for' is useful for is as a means of focusing attention. In education, to define our culture or brand, it is necessary to be able to articulate:

➢ what we stand for, our integrity
➢ what we demonstrate daily
➢ how we create an environment where people want to work
➢ how we work in partnership: staff, students, parents, governors and community
➢ how we communicate our key messages
➢ how we reward, in the broadest terms, effective performance.

We need to be clear about what we are trying to achieve and how the culture of our school helps or, indeed, prevents us from doing so. What follows are three insights from practice, one from the business world and two from the world of education. All three define the leadership or talent-development culture in their respective organisations.

Insights from practice: case example from the business world

Reckitt Benckiser plc is a major international company which has an organisational culture based on four cultural norms and values which are:

Leadership values:
➤ Achievement – 'We don't just aim high, we always aim to outperform.'
➤ Entrepreneurship – 'We allow daring ideas to thrive.'
➤ Ownership – 'We take the initiative to do what is needed.'
➤ Team Spirit – 'We work as one, united by common principles and attitudes.'

Leadership culture:
➤ Nothing is sacred – if there's a better way then let us do it.
➤ We use conflict appropriately – constructive conflict involving direct challenge at all levels which is non-hierarchical.
➤ We demand individuals who are willing to stand up and be counted.
➤ However, once agreed, we always deliver.
➤ We work with a common focus, not with common consensus.

Clearly, what the company is trying to do is to articulate what it stands for, to articulate what its integrity is and how it wants to deliver those values on a daily basis. The company articulates how staff, working in partnership, use the core values and core ways of working. This is a very precise and coherent description which helps focus attention on how the company wants to work and the culture the company has developed. In education, we may have differing values and a different emphasis but a similar clarity and eloquence would be a valuable ambition for schools to achieve.

Insights from practice: leadership culture in the primary school

At our nursery and primary school, we believe that our school culture is intrinsically linked with the culture in each classroom and that it is a powerful part of what goes on in our school. Our culture is positive, collaborative and professional. The concept of 'culture' relates to our shared beliefs, our values, our expectations and our behaviours. It is how our school 'feels' to members of the school community and to visitors. All aspects of 'how we do things around here' form our culture. We believe that our school is more than a number and that accountability through test scores, attendance figures and national rankings cannot tell our story and cannot detect the most important aspects of our school. Our culture can tell a more important story, that of how it feels to belong in and to learn in our school.

On joining the school, as head teacher, it was obvious that there was a negative culture: that of complacency, individualism and isolation both within school and with neighbouring schools. No one had a voice and children least of all; no one was involved with improvement planning. Corridors were noisy, self-centred places where staff were loath to take responsibility. The biggest advantage was most staff really cared and wanted this situation to change. It was a good time to address our core values and to move away from a culture which undermined any good practice.

Our culture determines what people focus on; it supports the importance of change and the capacity to improve. Our culture affects our motivation and motivation affects our achievements. In creating our culture, over six years, we focused on a widely shared and consistent sense of purpose and shared values. Most important and essential was developing trust and positive relationships between staff members, where people shared ideas, problems and solutions. We built a culture where we worked together to create a better school experience for everyone in our school community, a culture where there was energy, a sense of hope and possibility. This took time working positively to nurture the constructive aspects of our culture and working to eliminate the negative aspects. Our culture affects all aspects of our school, for example we established a concern for the importance of professional learning. We looked at how we celebrated it, how we encouraged and reinforced the importance of professional learning for all and focused on the importance of sharing ideas, practice and reflecting on practice

(Continues)

(Continued)

and taking a shared responsibility for our children's learning. This wouldn't have been possible without shared values, expectations and behaviours.

We played with slogans to try to capture our culture, for example 'together we can' became 'together I can' (i.e. taking responsibility with the support of others) but the use of a shared language to talk about our school and shared behaviours of how to act in our school became more important than elegant sayings to communicate our beliefs. We maintained a focus on: 'What is in the best interests of the children?' Reinforcing and celebrating our values became an important part of our school culture and slowly the core values, which were lived by everyone, could be experienced and felt just by walking through school. The positive effects on our school improvements were the establishment of:

➢ trust and confidence
➢ open and honest communication
➢ ready support
➢ high expectations
➢ appreciation and recognition
➢ caring and celebration
➢ involvement in decision making
➢ evaluation and experimentation
➢ collaboration and team working.

The biggest achievement and possibly the greatest influence were the first point, trust and confidence, and the last point, collaboration and team working. Culture is built through the everyday business of school life and while it can't be built without the evaluation, promotion and active creation by school leadership, it can't be maintained if all staff don't buy into it or recognise the importance of their role. A positive culture is difficult to build yet easy for someone to derail. If someone, in our case four people, demonstrates a lack of trust then other aspects of the culture topple like dominoes. Their behaviours did not follow the unwritten behaviour code for how we act and how we conduct business 'around here'. Awareness and commitment to culture building are more important than any other activity.

This case study demonstrates that if we are serious about school improvement and about attracting and retaining talented people, then our highest priority should be to sustain the school as an attractive workplace. If the culture is effective then the school will be attractive, energised and continuously improving. This takes time, energy and emotion. It is interesting to look at this school now; a new very inexperienced leader has been appointed as head and has been in place for a year. The culture is increasingly negative, morale is rock bottom and no core values are evident to anyone in the school community. No one is listened to and no one is involved in decision making. The school has reverted to being non-collegial and negative and this will be an obstacle to improvement. The cycle needs to begin again with an analysis and honest articulation of the current reality.

Developing an effective school culture is important for any school in order to develop and improve but it is absolutely vital if the school is to develop a strategic approach to managing talent. Such an approach begins with the school culture in order to attract the best talent, to promote the organisation as an 'employer of choice' and produce enhanced recruitment processes. The complexity of managing employee retention and engagement includes understanding the root causes of talent retention problems and the likelihood of top talent becoming future leaders. The key is to invest in talented people in order to optimise school achievements. Through performance reviews, staff can be motivated by learning opportunities. It is important to allow good performers to excel – this requires open and honest communication and trust. We will now look at a secondary example.

Insights from practice: leadership culture in the secondary school

Brentwich School is a specialist school of 1200 students – it is a church school with the following five values underpinning all our work: faith, justice, responsibility, truth and compassion. We see the key to improving the learning outcomes of all our students as high-quality leadership which can only be achieved by outstanding and talented leadership throughout the school. Our school achieved 'Leadership Partner School Specialist Status' in 2010 when we were awarded a second specialism, that of being a 'High Performing Specialist School' (HPSS), which focuses on excellence in leadership. Our first specialism

(Continues)

(Continued)

was for mathematics. Our school is one of approximately 50 schools nationally to be designated as a 'Leadership Partner School', working closely with the National College of School Leadership (NCSL). Leadership Partner Schools are defined as 'national hubs for the development of outstanding leadership and succession planning strategies'. The vision of our school is founded on the belief that the single most important thing that schools can do, as part of ensuring positive and successful student outcomes, is to ensure high-quality leadership and management. The contribution of leadership and management to school improvement is crucial. The vision encompasses planned and cohesive leadership development for all members of the community. In doing so, our school has moved on from a traditional leadership development and succession planning approach to adopt a talent-development framework which is based on creating a 'talent culture' where outstanding leaders develop and thrive.

As a school we have, over the past five years, created a school culture and a leadership culture that are interlinked and support each other. We seek to encourage all our students to strive for excellence in their learning and to take risks in their learning. We hope that by undertaking new and exciting challenges they will transform their learning; we see making mistakes as a learning opportunity and not repeating mistakes as a reflective process of continuous improvement. This is also the culture we have for developing our staff talent. We have well-established processes for mentoring and developing newly appointed teachers, both in their pedagogic skills but also in early stage leadership of their classroom and in contributing to the leadership of their subject and pastoral areas. We seek to identify embryonic leaders and nurture their development from an early stage. As well as induction programmes, we allocate mentors to all newly qualified staff to encourage a culture of individual professional reflection.

This process continues at middle management, where our culture is one of celebrating success and not dwelling on failures but asking the question 'What do we do next?' Each middle manager, as part of the annual review process, has the option of one of the senior leadership team acting as a leadership coach to help them reflect on their leadership approaches and to discuss plans for development. The senior leadership team also identify 'outstanding talent' and ensure they are given appropriate support.

The culture of the school is one of high achievement for all students. Pupils obviously do not achieve in the same way but will achieve in diverse ways at different levels. This is the same culture that we articulate and practise with all staff. We believe that all staff are professionals who want to do the best they can for all students and that means they should seek to continue to learn and develop. We seek to develop professionals who work:

> with responsibility
> with integrity
> as a team
> with the best interests of the children as a guiding value
> as lifelong learners.

We believe we have established a collaborative culture with high involvement and engagement from staff to deliver on our mission of creating the best learning opportunities for all our students.

The secondary example demonstrates a developing positive culture. Both school case studies demonstrate that organisational culture and leadership or talent-development culture cannot be isolated from each other. How we treat individuals and the values that underpin that treatment help to define the culture of the organisation. Newly appointed head teachers often find their most challenging task is that of changing or maintaining the positive culture of their school. Sustainable leadership can only be achieved if it is values-based and ethically driven.

Becoming a talent developer and engager

Central to developing a talent-management culture is for the leaders in a school to adopt an approach of becoming talent developers and engagers throughout the school. We would suggest that to achieve this, the following are key ideas:

> **Redefine the leadership culture** in order to recruit able and challenging individuals to take on current orthodoxies and move the organisation forward. Resist 'comfortable' appointments that fit into the current way of doing things and look for insightful change

agents who will look for new ways of doing things. The leadership approach should be to recruit 'the best of the best', not individuals who do not challenge us.

➤ **Focus on people-orientated relationships** – people are the key resource and you need to consider how all leaders in the school can maximise the contribution they give to and receive from their colleagues. The school is only as good as the talent it brings to bear on the learning process. First, the school needs to identify the talent; second, it needs to develop that talent; and third, it needs to engage and motivate those talented individuals.

➤ **Talent developers need courage** to take a risk on appointments where individuals come with different sets of experiences and skills from the norm that may lead to extraordinary performances. Diversity needs to be embraced as a positive way of achieving high performance. Talent managers also need to give staff challenging assignments where there is the possibility of failure as well as significant success – this takes courage.

➤ **Seek to be a coordinator or facilitator of a 'cabinet of talent' rather than the heroic leader.** It is a sobering but fulfilling role to be the organiser of highly competent leaders where you do not need to be seen as the expert or the authority on everything. Bringing out the best in the leadership talent in your organisation and motivating and developing those individuals should be a key performance indicator for evaluating senior leaders.

➤ **Challenge performance** – in being a talent developer and engager, the core task of encouraging high performance is to be matched by the ability to challenge average or poor performance. The ability to move the Bs to As is as difficult as removing the Ds. We need to think more about challenging performance and not just challenging underperformance.

➤ **Always go back to values** – talent is only a means to an end. Talent is not an end in itself but a means of achieving our core goals and purposes more effectively. Leaders need to focus on asking 'How does this set of people, with their skills and attributes, deliver our core purpose of transformational learning?' 'How could they be better aligned or organised to allow us to achieve our goals?' should be a constant question.

Talent is far easier to stifle than to grow and it is well that leaders understand what to avoid as well as what to encourage. The following reflection point looks at aspects of a school culture which will suppress potential leaders.

Refection point: how not to stifle talent

1. Do you allow people to be creative?
2. Do you allow the generation of ideas by others?
3. Are you, as a leader, fearful of the next talent being better than you?
4. Do you link performance with behaviour?
5. Do you have a low understanding of social interactions?
6. Are you able to judge the impact of actions and feelings?
7. Do you ensure challenge in the work of yourself and others?

Conclusion

How you behave says everything about what you value. The school culture is the heart and soul of the school organisation; it is the definition of the accepted way of life in that school. The culture is created by all staff but reflects the history of the group. Is the development of talent part of your school culture? If we want to bring about successful change, we need to focus on the culture of the school, to focus on the internal value systems.

Suggested further reading

Cheese, P., Thomas, R.J. and Craig, E. (2008) *The Talent Powered Organization.* London: Kogan Page.

Davies, B. and Brighouse, T. (2008) *Passionate Leadership.* London: Sage.

NCSL (2009) *What are we Learning about Identifying Talent – Evidence into Practice Guide.* Nottingham: NCSL.

Novak, J. (2009) 'Invitational leadership', in B. Davies (ed.) *Essentials of School Leadership.* London: Sage.

Talent assessment framework: where are you now? Talent culture

Rate yourself (in partnership discussion) on the following categories.

1 = not at all; 2 = only partially; 3 = to a degree; 4 = very often; 5 = completely

Values

Do we seek a talented and diverse workforce?	1	2	3	4	5
Are we trying to get the best out of all staff?	1	2	3	4	5
Can all staff deliver our values?	1	2	3	4	5

Personal qualities

Do we have staff who can challenge ideas?	1	2	3	4	5
Do staff use evaluations as a means to improve?	1	2	3	4	5
Can individuals take pride in others' success?	1	2	3	4	5

Working with others

Can staff effectively lead talented colleagues?	1	2	3	4	5
Are staff able to challenge performance in others?	1	2	3	4	5
Do most talented staff have personal modesty?	1	2	3	4	5

Strategic acumen

Does the school have a strategic talent development plan?	1	2	3	4	5
Do staff have an individual long-term personal development plan?	1	2	3	4	5

Those items you have rated '1' or '2' would need to be developed while those ranked '4' or '5' need to be celebrated and sustained. Those rated '3' warrant further reflection.

Chapter 9

School or system talent development?

This chapter considers:

➤ structures of systems leadership and collaboration
➤ the advantages of different organisational forms for talent management
➤ key issues of collaborative approaches to talent management.

One of the challenges with adopting a talent-management approach is that of scale. We need to consider whether an individual school is able to provide the managed development and the managed moves which are necessary to provide a systematic improvement process for talented staff. The answer is probably 'yes to a degree' but the full possibilities of a talent-management approach come with the scale of operation. Clearly, very large secondary schools have some potential to undertake effective programmes, pathways and processes but smaller schools and in particular primary schools need to collaborate to develop alternative forms of leadership development. Key to this is building relationships and networks to allow a more integrated talent-development approach to flourish. Different organisational forms which support the development of a talent-development approach can be seen and developed as follows:

1. **Informal collaboration** could be a school partnering with neighbouring schools to develop professional learning networks and talent-development networks. There is a long tradition of groupings to facilitate this organisation, especially in the primary school sector. Local authorities often encourage schools to work in groups of informal groupings and partnerships to share expertise and plan joint staff-development activities. This opens up the possibility of developing talent on a shared or group basis. In the following figure (Figure 9.1), three primary schools share ideas on some professional development activities:

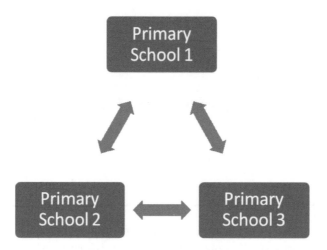

Figure 9.1 *Informal collaboration on specific topics*

2. A more formal development of this organisational collaboration is the development of **soft federations** where schools adopt a more strategic framework and agree a code of practice for working across the group in order to deliver the agreed objectives. However, each school retains its own governing body. This is represented in Figure 9.2:

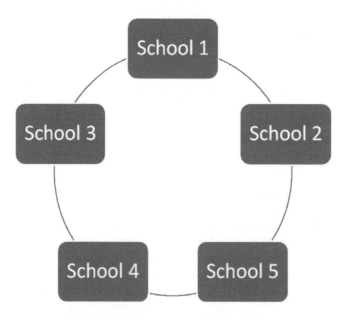

Figure 9.2 *Soft federations – individual governing bodies but sharing a common strategic focus and sharing planning*

3. A formal structure or partnership can be established which is known as a **hard federation**. Here, a school partners a neighbouring school or neighbouring schools and has one integrated governing body and administration and management system. Staff appointed to one school may have roles and responsibilities across several schools. In a hard federation, promotion and development can take place within the group of schools and planned experiences can be across more than one school. This is shown in Figure 9.3:

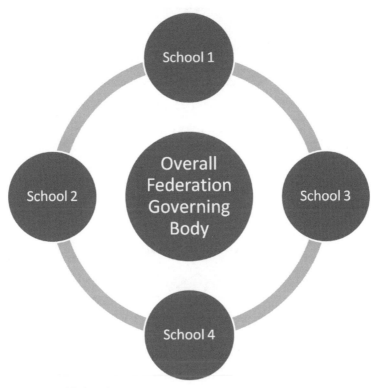

Figure 9.3   *Hard federations*

4. In the secondary sector, the establishment of **mini-schools within a larger school** framework facilitates the talent-development process by creating extensive leadership opportunities for the 'mini-school' leaders and potential leaders. An example of this is provided in Figure 9.4.

5. **All-through schools**, providing for 3–18 year olds, where an executive leader oversees both the primary and secondary phases, and also in some cases the special school provision, provide opportunities for talented leaders and potential leaders to take on

responsibilities earlier in their leadership journeys through the guidance of an executive head teacher.

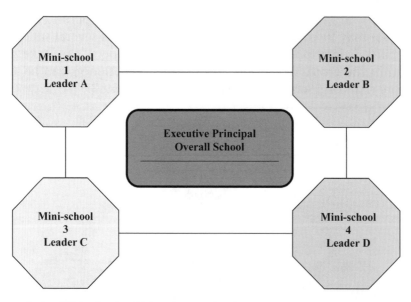

Figure 9.4 *Mini-schools within a larger school*

Executive Principal

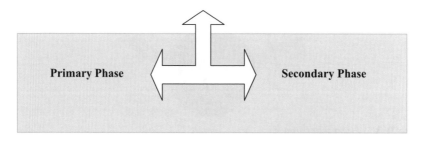

Figure 9.5 *All-through schools integrating primary and secondary phases*

6. A sixth organisational form is where a sponsor of a school sets up a significant number of schools under a **'brand'** or **'chain' approach** (Figure 9.6). This is based on a more business type model where the sponsoring organisation is able to see talent development taking place across different branches or schools in the group. The following insight from practice, of the Harris Federation of schools in South London, is a good example of this organisational form.

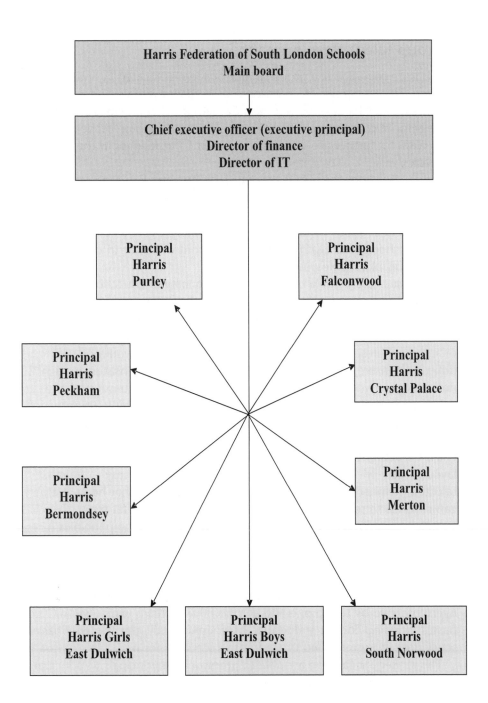

Figure 9.6 *A brand approach*

Insights from practice: the voice of the chief executive – group talent development

The Harris Federation is a group of nine academies located in South London. The academies are sponsored by Lord Harris of Peckham, Chairman and Chief Executive of the Carpetright chain, who is a serial benefactor of charitable causes. The group consists of nine academies, with plans for further growth to 12 and then 14 academies in the next few years.

It was clear from the outset that our rapid growth would place a premium on the identification and development of high-quality leaders. Furthermore, we wished to develop a consistent, high-quality and highly visible brand in South London, rather than simply create a collection of different schools, each with the Harris name but with little in common and possibly of variable quality.

Our desire to provide a consistently high quality of education made it possible to find a solution to the problem of developing an increasing number of excellent academy leaders within the context of a shrinking national leadership pool. We reasoned that if our academies each had different cultures, ethos, structures and systems, then it would be very difficult to ensure consistency between them. Without consistency, each new academy would be an experiment rather than an extension of an existing and successful formula, in the same way, for example (borrowing from our sponsor), that a new independent carpet shop might be compared to the establishment of a new branch of the market leading chain Carpetright. A new Carpetright store is recognisable in terms of its layout, stock, pricing, advertising, etc. and it is relatively easy to train a talented member of staff in one store in these things so that he or she can progress to run another store elsewhere. Schools are far more complex places, nevertheless we have found that the same principles hold true.

In establishing our group of schools, we chose to replicate the systems and procedures at the original Harris school, Harris CTC (now Harris City Academy Crystal Palace). This school has been established for 18 years, is oversubscribed by ten to one and around 80% regularly score five A–C passes including English and Maths. Most importantly, the academy has a set of policies, systems and procedures which work for us.

This strategy means we are able to promote vice principals to principal positions in new Harris academies sometimes faster than they would have been promoted in a standalone situation. This is because they are implementing tried-and-tested systems with which they are very familiar. Yet this is not a straight jacket. Common systems and policies operate in some key areas such as staffing structure, assessment, reporting and recording but other areas are determined locally. This is important not only to allow for further leadership development of successful candidates but also to attract strong outside candidates.

In order to support this process, we have established Harris as a hard federation, creating a single legal entity in the form of a registered charity. The group operates with a small central office comprising a CEO, a Finance Director, an ICT Director and a Projects Director. This central office and the CEO in particular exist to support and coach new principals. This can be seen as follows.

The federation has identified a group of future principals, vice principals and assistant principals from within the organisation and has made this known to the staff concerned. This also assists in terms of recruitment and retention. These staff are being developed and coached for promoted roles within the federation. The support involves placements and support projects in new academies whilst still being based in their substantive posts. Each of our academies stands to gain from this process, and so cooperation between them has been very good. Furthermore, where we appoint new principals from outside the group, we generally do so a year in advance of opening a new academy and we base the principal designate in an existing Harris academy during the preparatory year in order that they can absorb the Harris culture and structures.

What are the advantages of some of these organisational forms from a talent-management perspective?

First, building and enhancing the capability and capacity of talented staff is easier in larger organisational structures. Most significantly, where there are two or more schools in a group a systematic development framework can be established. Joint development activities can be organised, such as curriculum pairings of staff and benchmarking of practice. These types of professional leadership learning can more effectively take place in a collaborative setting. Professional development can be extended to take the form of planned staff moves in order for potential leaders to gain experience and promotion in different schools in the group. This allows school groups to develop their own talent pool through an integrated career development approach and was seen as a major area of activity for the head teachers in our research as shown in this statement:

> *What we want to do is to create internal frameworks for development and promotion as well as create effective links with our partner schools in order to have a structure for more and more staff at different levels to take on leadership roles in one of the partner schools.*

Second, the larger structures enable the expertise of experienced and talented leaders from one school to develop new leadership talent in another school. A good example of this is using experienced head teachers in one school as executive leaders or leadership coaches to support newly appointed leaders in another school. It is well accepted that there is a national shortage of leaders and a reluctance of potential leaders to undertake leadership roles – this approach allows these potential leaders to 'step up' to the role within a supportive framework. Capacity building is a major issue here. As one executive head teacher articulated:

> *They wouldn't have chosen to be Heads if they had not been in the Federation but they are very talented people and this has given them the opportunity to take on the post with support.*

This is a recurrent theme in many of our research interviews as witnessed by this statement:

> *Both the colleagues who are leading our two schools as headteachers at the moment may well not have been attracted to those jobs if they thought they were going to run the whole shooting match, but I think because I was available and able to use my experience to support them and almost be like the permanent critical friend, I think that has enabled them to take on those roles and are now able to do the things that they are really good at.*

The site head teachers also saw the benefits of having a supportive executive head teacher as shown in these two statements:

> *One of the things with me, I lacked self-confidence in some ways to take on the new role so I thought it would be good to have somebody working with me and supporting me. I knew I could work with the Executive Head. It is like having a stepping stone into Headship. You know it's almost easing you in although I knew by becoming a head in a brand*

new school there were going to be other huge pressures. When I got into the role, initially I was co-leader with someone with immense experience. It enabled me to focus on some key issues and let someone more experienced deal with others.

So we would look at what needed to be done, we would work out targets, together we would work out action points for each target. This was not me being told what to do but co-constructing what we should actually be doing. We had action points for every half term, for almost every fortnight at first, and then we would go back and review what I had achieved. Later it became broader in approach and based on quality assurance.

Third, economies of scale across two or more schools provide considerable advantages. All the head teachers in our study talked about having a central finance officer to achieve economies of provision and avoid duplicating systems and this also was the case for a joint provision and strategy for information technology. The participants in our research also mentioned that the ability to undertake joint staff development was effective as was using the whole group as a means of providing staff with varied developmental pathways in different schools in the group. Schools in the secondary field were able to have good heads of departments working across two or more schools – this meant that shortages in one school could be remedied through such an approach. For example, at departmental level one head teacher reported:

Across the two schools we had two weak Heads of Maths but we found an outstanding Head of Maths in the third school who was ready to move into senior management. We made her an Assistant Head but she is also the Head of Maths across the schools in the group. We are trying to do that more and more. We are growing our own Advanced Skills Teachers and we are appointing them to leadership roles. The idea is to create an in-house advisory team.

Insights from practice: collaboration across six primary schools

Initially, our group of six neighbouring schools came together in order to secure funding for professional development which was not available to one school alone. This was not the best start. It became apparent very quickly that four of the schools were committed to collaboration

(Continues)

(Continued)

and could see the future benefits especially in the potential opportunities for leadership development. All schools took part in the project while funding was available. The project was successful, mainly because of the head teacher who led it but relationships between the schools were only effective in the four cases. These were the schools who shared common values, were willing to discuss difficulties and celebrate joint achievements. These four leaders believed that collaboration was better than competition between schools. This trust was not experienced with the other two schools.

Because these four schools had worked together on the first project, each taking on active roles and supporting each other, it was easy to make the decision to work together to find a solution to the shared problem of developing an approach for managing talented staff. We developed a working group to establish the criteria for leadership behaviours. In each school, we used this framework for colleagues' self-evaluation and for leadership teams to identify potential leaders in their own school. The collaborative evaluation we had on the implementation of this framework was very effective and led to further improvements. But we didn't stop there. Together we worked out pathways and opportunities for colleagues on the leadership journey. This included:

➤ a school-based masters course
➤ job shadowing across the four schools
➤ shared improvement projects
➤ a leadership journal group where incidents were discussed and practice evaluated
➤ one School Business Manager (SBM) coaching a newly appointed SBM in one of the partnership schools
➤ a member of the learning support staff leading a partnership group to introduce a new initiative across the four schools.

Staff taking on these leadership opportunities are coached by an experienced leader in the group. We wanted to establish a placement for a term for two members of staff to work in different roles in the different context of a school in the partnership but so far this hasn't been agreed by governors. The difficulty is the fact that these teachers are classroom based. However, we are undaunted and will continue to work together with the now established processes and will work together to find the funding which would enable potential leaders to have the opportunity to work in each other's contexts.

Following the successful achievement of masters accreditation, two colleagues are going on to work for the National Professional Qualification for Headship. The support they give each other is exemplary. In evaluating the impact of our joint project, we are all agreed that we have been able to give colleagues more relevant and context-based learning opportunities than we could have done alone. By involving the governors, there is a trust building between the schools whiches will support the joint placement of two colleagues as acting heads in one of our schools following the illness of the head teacher in post.

The local authority is now very interested in this project for leadership development which is rooted in professional practice and wishes to disseminate our good practice across the county. As a consequence, one of our four head teachers is now on the local authority working team for sustaining leadership.

Insights from practice: talent management across secondary schools

Recruiting, identifying, utilising and developing talent is the critical factor in improving schools at all levels and especially in Thurrock, an area where recruitment and retention are deeply problematic. Traditional school hierarchies and leadership roles often hinder the development and the most productive use of talented people, hence an increasing number of individual schools are rethinking these roles and introducing either flatter hierarchies or, in some cases, new imaginative models of school leadership. However, the opportunity to develop exceptional and able people is significantly enhanced where they are able to work in a number of schools which collaborate on developing talent. This also has the facility of enabling the colleagues to experience different contexts.

Such an opportunity has presented itself in Thurrock where four schools are working together to develop talent. To cite one example, the executive head teacher of Gable Hall School, a very successful high-performing secondary school, had recruited an exceptional male PE teacher in January 2000. Early on, he demonstrated significant leadership potential and in common with all staff, he met with a member of the Strategic Leadership Team to help him consider his aspirations and a suitable career pathway. He engaged in an intensive

(Continues)

(Continued)

programme of Continuing Professional Development (CPD), delivered both internally and externally, and was prepared for and promoted to the next stage of his leadership development programme. In doing so, he occupied a number of positions where he could practise and utilise his newly developed knowledge and skills and, importantly, prepare for the next stage. By 2007, he was an assistant head teacher, showing significant headship potential. However, opportunities to develop further were limited in Gable Hall and he was likely to be disadvantaged by only having worked in one school in one context.

As a National Leader of Education supporting a challenging school in difficulty in Thurrock, the head teacher was able both to help the school, and to overcome the barrier to the talented person's continuing development by seconding him and a female colleague in a similar position at William Edwards, his other school, which was also in difficulties, as acting deputy head teachers for almost a year. Both talented people excelled and were mentioned several times in HMI's reports as being key factors in the improvements the school had made since his previous visits. Both were provided with the opportunity to put what they had learned into practice in a different environment and to prepare for the next level of leadership. Both undertook extensive CPD and were mentored and coached throughout. Both were energised, motivated and had developed and utilised their immense talents as a result of the experience. Subsequently, the very able PE teacher was successful in his application for a substantive deputy headship post at William Edwards School.

Since then, another challenging school, soon to become an academy, has joined the collaborative and in September five more talented people will undertake further training and development cross-institution, which the head teacher firmly believes will bring significant benefits to each school, help retain these key people in the local community and impact positively on standards.

Key issues for successful implementation of collaborative approaches to talent management

In our research interviews with head teachers, a number of factors emerged when they expressed how they had built successful cross-organisations and relationships.

Organisational trust

The individual personalities of the participants clearly also have an impact and there needs to be a high degree of mutual trust and honest communication, as shown in this comment:

> You need to really know the other partners, you need to trust them absolutely and so they're actually articulating the same values and building the same ethos.

This also links to our earlier chapter about values and strategy. It is very unlikely that sustainable partnership working would be possible if schools did not have similar or complementary values and strategic frameworks and objectives. This is particularly important in trying to establish a value system that builds a framework for 'the common good' rather than a competitive approach that pits one school against another. The establishment of school partnerships needs to pay a great deal of attention to establishing strong personal and organisational understanding and respect for effective talent management to be possible.

Working with known people

Schools where leaders had worked together on other projects and initiatives obviously found it easier to work together on talent-management approaches. One interesting finding from our research related to executive headship. Executive head teachers talked of working with previous deputy head teachers who had been part of the culture of the sponsoring school and had already understood the culture and the ways of working and had established a sense of trust with the executive head teacher. Thus, cross-institutional working was based on previous experience and understanding. One executive head teacher commented:

> Both site headteachers were my deputies even though we went to external interview, so that was interesting. What we found is that it works because you get this single message coming through and everybody knows what they're buying into.

Speed of implementation

The speed with which the new approaches to collaboration can be set up is important. While it is necessary to spend time building up understanding and trust, it is important that this does not become an 'endless talking shop'. It is important to create a sense of momentum to move forward initiatives such as talent management. In terms of leadership, there is a need to assess the situation and confront critical supporters and 'blockers' and move to suitable action for improvement. Two key issues were seen to be working to ensure that any initial problems of moving to a talent-management framework and winning over staff were solved, to enable them to 'buy in' and be committed to the new culture. This is shown in the quote: 'Getting everyone on side as soon as possible was a key priority'. The ability to accept and manage conflict and personal challenge was quoted by nearly all leaders as something they had to do to make things happen quickly.

Focus

The head teachers saw one of their roles as keeping a focus on talent development for future leaders and not letting joint work slip into broadly based 'feel good' professional development activities. One head teacher said they tried to ensure:

that we didn't get distracted by the other things but focused on identifying leadership talent by making sure it wasn't wasted; we needed to be proactive to make sure something happened for those individuals.

Another head teacher took the view:

We have limited resources so we need to make sure they count. If we are developing leadership we need to put the money where we get maximum return. That return is excellent leaders making a difference to children's learning.

This focus and a sense of priority was a common theme as witnessed by the following research interview comment:

At the end of the day it is about the performance of the children, it is about building a moral purpose of education. That fundamental moral purpose is that these young people have got to get the best possible opportunities. We need to develop leaders who can deliver that as a priority for the organisation.

Capacity for continuous leadership improvement

If talent management is to work across a grouping of schools, it is important to assess what the leadership capacity is in each school. We need to ask if there is an open and critical dialogue regarding leadership skills and to ask what the development needs are for individuals. The challenge is not just with underperforming schools but also schools that are 'cruising' or 'strolling' and do not see the need to change and develop to build and enhance their leadership capacity through a talent-management approach. While head teachers clearly took the responsibility for rapid improvement of an underperforming school in the short term, they saw their role not just as immediate remedial action. This is demonstrated by the following quote:

> There were a lot of immediate problems but as well as sorting them out the key task was building leadership capacity to improve and keep on improving in the long term.

Leading and managing powerful personalities

The relationships between leaders in partnership working are critical. This can be very difficult in voluntary partnership groupings. It can also be challenging in schools which are part of a sponsored group of schools.

> They are very competitive but they've all been appointed and it's all been made clear that this is a federation; we are expected to work together and if you don't want to do that then don't come here. So that's the first thing. Secondly the sponsor is very committed to the federation and he is a major figure and they know that he's committed to it so I have that behind me supporting, which is really really good. The sponsor wants a federation, he wants us to work together so that's a big help. Without the sponsor's support I think it would be a lot more difficult.

And:

> They are competitive but I don't find that a problem, they're quite strong willed and I'm quite strong willed and you know if it's a question of taking people aside and saying 'look for the benefit of the federation you need to do this' then if they say 'I'm not', which has happened once or twice, then it's down to the sponsor and he usually supports me and says 'yes you need to do this'.

Future issues regarding size of partnerships

What is the ideal size of partnership working to share good practice and build innovative and creative solutions without being too large and bureaucratic? This seems to be one of the key questions for the future development of talent-management approaches. Schools which had started from one school partnering another and then taken on one or two additional schools had different perspectives from school groups which from the start had envisaged having a chain of schools.

The schools that had partnered with another local school and envisaged others joining them made these comments:

> I know how long it takes with these things from an expression of interest to working through to a functional partnership; it takes about 18 months to get going, so that's why I know we should be starting now to expand. We want other schools to join us. The interesting thing is people say well how many schools can there be in a partnership and make it still be effective? I can't imagine it could be more than four or five because then you can't do the operational and keep involved.

And:

> I mean we're talking with the colleagues about a fourth secondary in the trust and I think that's it, I think four has the balance between being the right economies of scale; it gives you the whole fabric around succession planning and training that you've got within enough local schools, but I think it still enables you to work with people on an individual basis. So you know if we were working in a model where there were three or four schools but they were all over the country, I don't think that would work for me because I don't think I'm ready to be an administrator.

But in the academy sector, the chief executive of a group of academies made this comment:

> I wanted to stay with six schools until we got them consolidated. But the sponsor has a target of a dozen; I think we can probably manage twelve schools but it just depends on how we sequence them.

Clearly, the academy groups believe they can run chains of 12–20 academies without taking on the bureaucratic features of small local authorities – this, it would seem, is a tall order.

Conclusion: talent development: the way forward

If we are to be able to provide high-quality individuals to direct our schools in the future, talent development should be a leadership and management priority. Talent management can take place in one school and certainly both primary and secondary schools in our research have demonstrated that quite clearly. The challenge that schools face however is that to obtain the full benefits of such an approach with a number of schools is desirable. We have shown in this chapter that informal or formal groupings of schools provide the opportunity to maximise the opportunities for extensive and significant talent development. The implication for school leaders is that they should clearly be well-networked leaders to be able to draw on wider resources and partnerships in the development of talent.

Suggested further reading

Hopkins, D. (2007) *Every School a Great School*. Buckingham: Open University Press.
NCSL (2006) *School Leaders Leading the System: System Leadership in Practice*. Nottingham: NCSL.

Talent assessment framework: school or system talent development?

Rate yourself (in partnership discussion) on the following categories.

1 = not at all; 2 = only partially; 3 = to a degree; 4 = very often; 5 = completely

Values

Do you think you have the responsibility for the success of all schools in your area?   1 2 3 4 5

How far is your partnership with other schools based on collaboration and shared values?   1 2 3 4 5

Personal qualities

Does your leadership team have extensive and effective networking skills?   1 2 3 4 5

How do you develop these skills in potential leaders?   1 2 3 4 5

Working with others

Do your support staff operate partnerships with staff in other schools?   1 2 3 4 5

Are your potential leaders able to instigate and take part in joint   1 2 3 4 5
projects with other schools?

Strategic acumen

Do you have a shared plan to develop talent across schools in your area?   1 2 3 4 5

Have you identified economies of scale which could follow strategic collaboration?   1 2 3 4 5

Those items you have rated '1' or '2' would need to be developed while those ranked '4' or '5' need to be celebrated and sustained. Those rated '3' warrant further reflection.

The Way Forward

Chapter 10

An integrated talent-management model for schools

Whale and minnows: a new paradigm for talent management in your school

Figure 10.1 *Whale and minnows*

Organisations in the education sector are traditionally in practice large bureaucracies which are slow to respond to external changes and slow to respond to the internal staffing dynamics of the school. As such, we could consider them to be like whales, large and magnificent maybe

171

but difficult to manoeuvre and slow to turn and respond. A more desirable image may be of a shoal of minnows which are linked with a neural net so that they are able to swim together in the same direction but are able to swiftly adjust and change as circumstances necessitate. This image of a shoal symbolises a school with a number of talented staff who each have their own development pathways and set of skills but are linked through their school's values and strategy. This staff group would be able to move and adapt quickly. Schools therefore need to replace bureaucratic staff development systems with more personalised talent-development systems. Just as schools are moving or have moved to personalised learning for students, they also need to move to personalised talent-management approaches for their staff. We need to consider how we get a talent-management approach which will enhance the development of talented individuals who are highly motivated and entrepreneurial but who still work collaboratively within the framework of the school's values and strategy. In this final chapter, we would like to develop some ideas for our reader to consider, along with their colleagues, before we bring together some of our own ideas.

The strategic importance of talent

Talent management is the process through which schools anticipate and meet the needs for key individuals in their organisation for the future. Talent-led schools have distinctive leadership which has the skills and abilities to produce transformational learning for students. The strategic question for schools is whether they are reliant on always buying in that new talent by recruiting from outside or whether they give a high importance to developing their own talent. This book has argued throughout that schools should put a premium on developing their own talent because we are entering an era of a talent shortage with the demographic time bomb of the retirement of a very large proportion of the leadership cadre in our schools. Thus, the strategic importance of this book is to encourage the reader to prioritise talent development and talent management as a means of sustainable school development.

The need to embrace diversity

There is always the danger of appointing people who 'look like us, think like us and dress like us' because we feel comfortable with them. What we should want to achieve is not conformity or conflict but diversity. Individuals from different backgrounds, cultures and experiences bring a diversity of perspectives which can make a major contribution to thinking differently and seeking innovative solutions to the educational challenges that the school faces. When considering talent development, the political comment of the Obama administration in the USA drawn from the Lincoln presidency of a 'cabinet of all the talents' is one to which we should aspire. We need a broad collection of talents to maximise the potential of the pedagogic and intellectual capital of the school. This should be a priority in talent development.

To make talent management work, you need to remember: signals, symbols and systems

- ➤ Signals: Explicit communications
- ➤ Symbols: Personal behaviour
- ➤ Systems: Measurements and rewards

Signals

Communication regarding what we regard as high performance, what we expect of our staff, how we reward excellence and how we develop talent should be part of an ongoing dialogue and communication strategy about developing and sustaining a high-performing talent pool and subsequently a high-performing school.

Symbols

Talent management has to be lived by the leaders in the school. If we define appropriate leadership behaviours, then leaders must demonstrate them by their actions and not just in what they say. What one shows by doing is vital – the personal symbolic acts that the leader performs become the reality of leadership in the school. Talk is cheap. If behaviour supports the talk, then it is believed; otherwise, it is dismissed.

Systems

If you tell your staff that they are to be assessed by new individualised performance-management approaches and systems but then you hold them accountable by collective performance and pay systems for process performance, you build conflict and distrust into the system. System inputs, processes, outcomes and rewards need to be aligned.

Everyone's responsibility

It is worth reminding ourselves that talent development should not be confined to those at the top of an organisation or one senior leader who is responsible for staff development. While in primary schools it is likely to be the head teacher who takes the responsibility and in secondary the head or deputy head, it is important that the culture of developing talent is shared and dispersed. It should be that individuals in coordinating or leadership roles see the critical importance of their own professional learning and development and their responsibility to develop their colleagues to enhance the leadership capacity of the school. It should be in the mindset of 'doing with' and not 'doing to' that we are able to build engagement with others.

The challenge of engagement – alignment and motivation

If talent management is going to move from a formal process to the way the school operates in terms of talent development as one of the values and cultural ways of doing things, then quite clearly engaging staff in the process is vital so they are aligned to the values and goals of the school and are motivated to contribute. However, it is important to consider different segments of the school's staff. Those with different roles and responsibilities and at different stages of their careers need to have different patterns of development and support. As we saw earlier with the nine-box grid, the A, B, C and D individuals will need different strategies applied to and with them. Treating everyone fairly and transparently is a must but treating everyone the same will not give us the individualised process which is necessary. Engaging individuals in a positive learning culture should be a constant focus for the ongoing improvement of the school.

The importance of learning and skills development

It is worth reminding ourselves of the key dimensions of leadership that we are trying to develop in talent leaders:

Values:

➤ Trust
➤ Truth
➤ Respect

Working with others:

➤ Communication
➤ Care and concern
➤ Credibility
➤ Support and challenge

Personal qualities:

➤ Resilience
➤ Confidence
➤ Risk taking
➤ Self-motivation
➤ Intellectual curiosity

Strategic acumen:

➤ Create strategic intent
➤ Shape the future
➤ Make things happen
➤ Make connections
➤ See the big picture

It is important to focus and re-focus on what the leadership talents are that we are trying to develop and how we can continue to emphasise the desirable activities we want to construct to enable us to develop those talents.

The way forward: an integrated talent management model

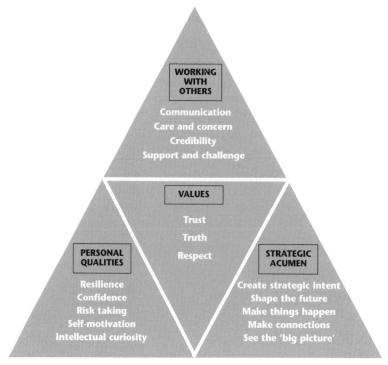

Figure 10.2 *Key dimensions of leadership*

The management of talent is driven by performance-management and school-evaluation processes, which enable the identification of talent. In turn, this informs aspects of professional learning in order to ensure the development of that talent. As we have stressed throughout this book, the whole is underpinned by strong core values, shared and acted out by all in the school community. The core values drive how people behave and drive what is considered to be important in the school. Without trust, respect and honesty, the system breaks down. We have also established that strategy is vital in order to improve. The strategy for the school should also be understood and owned by those making it happen. It influences, and is influenced by, the processes for school evaluation, school-improvement planning and professional learning. The operational plan is at the heart of the system – this should be developed and enabled by all in the school community, and should reflect the voices of the children and parents as well as the staff and governors. The school-improvement plan is driven by the strategy and informed by school-evaluation data and the impact of professional learning and performance-management outcomes. The performance-management process is clearly linked as a two-way process with the school-evaluation processes, the professional-learning process and the school-improvement plan. If it is effective both as a process in its own right and as a system to drive talent management, it will influence the professional learning opportunities provided. The talent-management process should be steered by both the performance-management and school-evaluation outcomes. The model is easy to picture and it is easy to reflect on it and conclude that your school does all of this, but take a few minutes to consider whether the talent-management process in your school really is integrated with these other key processes. We learn by making choices and honestly reflecting on those choices.

Reflection point

➤ Do your core values really affect school processes?

➤ Are the core values seen in the practice of these processes?

➤ Is the school-improvement plan informed by the school's strategy, the school's self-evaluation data, the professional-learning outcomes and the performance reviews?

➤ Do your school-evaluation data and your performance-management outcomes drive the talent-management process?

➤ Would potential leaders in your school recognise that their identified needs are developed through your professional-learning provision?

➤ Is professional learning really an outcome of the strategic direction, the improvement plan, the performance-management objectives and talent processes?

A school's capacity to improve is vital and 9 areas to be addressed can be established. The processes involved in our model are all key functions of that capacity to improve. The robustness of these systems to support development and learning are paramount. The first seven indicators are seen in Figure 10.3.

The ability of the governors to act in their capacity of critical friend and the evidence of ways in which earlier weaknesses have been addressed are the final indicators of a school's capacity to improve. Talent management is about creating the influential and innovative leadership team needed for the future. Just as with children, what is important is not what a person is but what they might become. Management enables an institution to operate effectively, and is concerned with orderly structures, monitoring functions and ensuring work gets done. It is about being organised and without this organisation, the processes cannot be established. But leadership enables an organisation to function well, it is about personal and interpersonal behaviour, a focus on the future and about change. 'In the end it is important to remember that we cannot be what we need to become by remaining what we are' (De Pree, 1989). A developmental model for talent management is forward-looking, focused and selective and centred on shared evaluation.

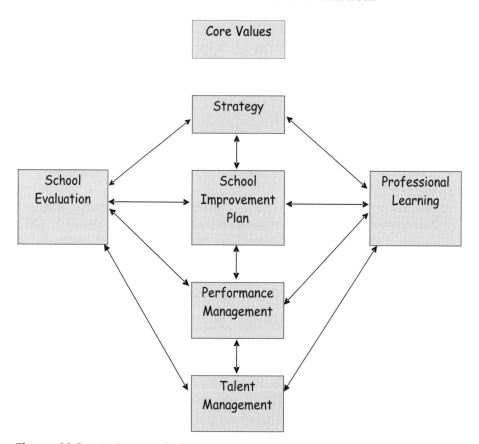

Figure 10.3   *An integrated talent-management process model*

Stages in enacting talent management

We believe a talent-management approach would involve a staged process which we outline in the following taxonomy of 10 points. Readers may wish to use this taxonomy to consider practice in their own school – in the following exercise, we provide a proforma to do this. It is worth considering that this is not a 'pick and mix menu' but all elements need to be present for a fully functioning talent-management process to happen in schools.

1. Define values and strategy

We made the obvious point in Chapters 1 and 2 that if you do not know where you are going and you do not know the values that underpin your organisation, then it will be very difficult, if not impossible, to recruit and develop leadership talent to drive your organisation forward. How well schools do this is critical to the whole talent process.

2. Establish rigorous performance evaluation

Given that performance management is statutory in the UK, one would expect this to be in place in all schools. Our research suggests it is patchy and the rigorous performance evaluation is not present in a significant proportion of schools. This needs to be in place because if 'you don't know what you have got', how can you develop it? The focus in school improvement has often focused on challenging underperformance – while this is necessary, it is not sufficient. Challenging satisfactory teachers and leaders to be good and the good to be outstanding is a significant factor in creating high-performing schools. This is often very difficult as the 'cruising' or 'strolling' school with good results does not always see the need to challenge, change and improve.

3. Distinguish between performance and potential

We have given considerable attention in this book to emphasising the difference between performance and potential. However, in our research we have found this to be a weak feature in many schools. Highlighting the potential for leadership needs greater attention within the school system.

4. Talent development

This means that staff within the school are proactive in their own development and in taking a proactive responsibility for developing the talent of their colleagues for whom they are responsible. It moves away from traditional models of staff development to seizing the initiative to enhance the long-term leadership capacity of the school.

5. Establish powerful professional learning

Talent development can only happen if there is powerful professional learning throughout the organisation. Professional learning needs to be part of the culture and given priority if the school is to be strategically sustainable as an improving learning institution.

6. Establish the architecture to support talent development

Talent management does not just happen because the leaders in the school think it is a good idea and want it to happen. In establishing structures and processes for talent development, schools establish the architecture to ensure this happens.

7. Establish a talent-management culture

Becoming a talent developer and engager links into the nature of the school culture. This culture believes that all staff can improve and believes in proactive leadership which challenges performance. Does your school have a culture where appointable and outstanding individuals challenging what you do is the norm or something that they avoid? The cultural underpinning of talent management strengthens much of what we are trying to do in the talent field.

8. Working within a wider system

A systems approach would suggest that to maximise the potential of talent management collaboration or integration with other schools would yield considerable benefits. Leaders should seek opportunities to do this.

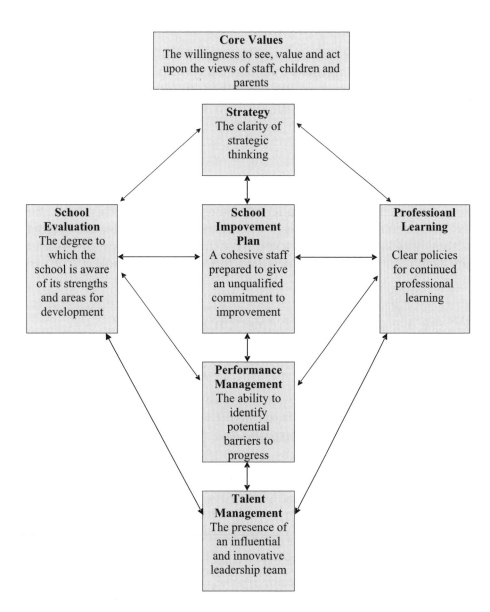

Figure 10.4 *Indicators of a school's capacity to improve (based on our integrated talent-management model).*

9. Integrate talent management into whole-school processes

Figure 10.2 and the commentary that goes with it demonstrate the need for talent management to be integrated into the whole leadership and management structure and not to be a bolt-on activity. Only if this takes place will there be the opportunity for sustainable success.

A final thought

For the longer-term sustainability of schools, we need to address this key issue of developing leadership talent. We hope this book has assisted in that debate. It might be interesting to consider the original activity in Chapter 1 to see if you have different scores or understanding now you have read and acted on the ideas in the book.

Where are you now with talent management?

For each statement below, indicate how accurately the statement describes your school. 1 indicates 'rarely' on a graded scale to 5 which indicates 'always'.

1. We have a clearly articulated set of core values.   1 2 3 4 5
2. The values are demonstrated in daily behaviours.   1 2 3 4 5
3. We have a strategic plan which includes talent development.   1 2 3 4 5
4. We have an effective performance management   1 2 3 4 5
   process which supports the identification of talent.
5. We are able to discriminate between current   1 2 3 4 5
   performance and future potential of staff.
6. We can map the behaviours, skills and attitudes   1 2 3 4 5
   which need to be developed in potential leaders.   1 2 3 4 5
7. Our professional learning includes specific   1 2 3 4 5
   opportunities to develop leadership potential.
8. We have pathways, programmes and processes to   1 2 3 4 5
   facilitate the development of talent.
9. Our culture enables the celebration of everyone's talents.   1 2 3 4 5
10. We work in partnership with others to develop   1 2 3 4 5
    talent in a more effective way.

References

Adair, J. (1990) *Leadership and Motivation*. London: Kogan Page.

Adair, J. (2006) *Effective Leadership Development*. London: Kogan Page.

Barth, R. (1990) *Improving Schools from Within*. San Francisco, CA: Jossey-Bass.

Benzia, T., Burnet D., Oliver, C. and Paxton, R. (2001) *Lateral Leadership Stages of Growth: From Trust to Breakthrough Thinking*. White Paper. Lateral Leadership LLC. http//www.itcoaches.org/pdf/Lateral%20 Leadership%20White%Paper.pdf

Brubaker, D.L. and Colbe, L.D. (2005) *The Hidden Leader*. Thousand Oaks, CA: Corwin Press.

Bruce, A. and Pepitone, J.S. (1999) *Motivating Employees*. New York: McGraw Hill.

Byham, W.C., Smith, A.B. and Paese, M.J. (2002) *Grow Your own Leaders*. London: FT Press.

Carter, K. and Halsall, R. (2001) 'Teacher research for school improvement', in R. Halsall (ed.) *Teacher Research for School Improvement*. Buckingham: Open University Press.

Cheese, P., Thomas, R.J. and Craig, E. (2008) *The Talent Powered Organization*. London: Kogan Page.

CIPD (2006) *Talent Management: Understanding the Dimensions*. London: CIPD.

CIPD (2007) *Talent: Strategy, Management, Measurement*. London: CIPD.

Collins, J. (2001) *Good to Great*. London: Random House Business Books.

Cross, A. (2007) *Talent Management Pocketbook*. Alresford, Hants: Management Pocketbooks Ltd.

Davies, B. (2007) *Developing Sustainable Leadership*. London: Sage.

Davies, B. (2011) *Leading the Strategically Focused School*. London: Sage.

Davies, B. (ed.) (2009) *Essentials of School Leadership*. London: Sage.

Davies, B. and Brighouse, T. (2008) *Passionate Leadership*. London: Sage.

Davies, B. and Brundrett, M. (2010) *Developing Successful Leadership*. New York: Springer.

Davies, B. and Davies, B.J. (2009) 'Strategic leadership', in B. Davies (ed.) *Essentials of School Leadership*. London: Sage.

Davies, B.J. (2004) 'An investigation into the development of a strategically focused primary school', EdD thesis, University of Hull.

Deal, T. and Peterson, K.D. (1999) *Shaping School Culture*. San Francisco, CA: Jossey-Bass.

De Pree, M. (1989) *Leadership is an Art*. New York: Dell.

Dweck, C.S. (2000) *Self-theories: their Role in Motivation, Personality and Development*. Philadelphia, PA: Psychology Press.

Evans, L. (2003) 'Leadership role: morale, job satisfaction and motivation', in L. Kydd, L. Anderson and W. Newton (eds) *Leading People and Teams in Education*. London: PCP.

Gay, M. and Sims, D. (2006) *Building Tomorrow's Talent*. Milton Keynes: AuthorHouse.

Gilbert, I. (2002) *Essential Motivation in the Classroom*. London: Routledge.

Goleman, D. (2000) 'Leadership that gets results', *Harvard Business Review*, March/April.

Handscombe, G. and MacBeath, J. (2003) *The Research Engaged School*. Chelmsford: Essex County Council.

Hay Group (2005) *Talent Management: What the Best Organisations Actually Do*. London: Hay Group.

Hay Group (2008) *Rush to the Top*. London: Hay Group.

Higham, R., Hopkins, D. and Matthews, P. (2009) *Systems Leadership in Practice*. Maidenhead: Open University Press.

Hopkins, D. (2007) *Every School a Great School.* Buckingham: Open University Press.

Hughes, R.L. and Beatty, K.C. (2005) *Becoming a Strategic Leader.* San Francisco, CA: John Wiley.

Jackson, M.C. (2003) *Systems Thinking: Creative Holism for Managers.* Chichester: John Wiley.

Jones, J., Jenkin, M. and Lord, S. (2006) *Developing Effective Teacher Performance.* London: PCP.

Josephson, M. (1990) *Making Ethical Decisions.* Marina del Ray, CA: The Josephson Institute of Ethics.

Kouzes, J.M. and Posner, B.Z. (1999) *Encouraging the Heart: A Leader's Guide to Rewarding and Recognizing Others.* San Francisco, CA: Jossey-Bass.

Leithwood, K., Day, C., Sammons, P., Harris, A. and Hopkins, D. (2006) *Seven Strong Claims about Successful School Leadership.* Nottingham: NCSL.

Maslow, A.H. (1954) *Motivation and Personality.* New York: Harper Row.

Michaels, E., Hadfield-Jones, H. and Axelrod, B. (2001) *The War for Talent.* Boston, MA: Harvard Business School Press.

Nanus, B. (1992) *Visionary Leadership.* San Francisco, CA: Jossey-Bass.

NCSL (2008) *Review of the Landscape: Leadership and Leadership Development.* Nottingham: NCSL.

NCSL (2009) *What are we Learning about Identifying Talent – Evidence into Practice Guide.* Nottingham: NCSL.

Novak, J. (2009) 'Invitational leadership', in B. Davies (ed.) *Essentials of School Leadership.* London: Sage.

Ott, J.S. (1989) *The Organizational Culture Perspective.* Pacific Grove, CA: Brooks/Cole.

Peters, T. (2005) *Talent: Develop it, Sell it, Be it.* London: Dorling Kindersley.

Rhodes, C.P., Bateman, J. and Farr, J. (2005) 'Partnership or parallelism? Modelling university support teacher research in schools', *Professional Development Today,* 25–30.

Robertson, A. and Abbey, G. (2001) *Clued Up: Working Through Politics and Complexity*. London: Pearson Education.

Rogers, E.M. (1995) *Diffusion of Innovations*, 4th edn. New York: The Free Press.

Thorne, K. and Pellant, A. (2007) *The Essential Guide to Managing Talent*. London: Kogan Page.

Index

LIBRARY, UNIVERSITY OF CHESTER